Meet Me Where I Am, Lord

Emilie Barnes

HARVEST HOUSE PUBLISHERS

EUGENE, OREGON

Cover design by Terry Dugan Design, Minneapolis, Minnesota

Cover photo © Harrison Eastwood/Digital Vision/Getty Images

Harvest House Publishers has made every effort to trace ownership of all poems and quotes. In the event of a question arising from the use of any poem or quote, we regret any error and will be pleased to make any necessary correction in future editions of this book.

MEET ME WHERE I AM, LORD
formerly Minute Meditations for Women
Copyright © 1999 by Harvest House Publishers
Published in 2006 by Harvest House Publishers
Eugene, Oregon 97402

Library of Congress Catalog-in-Publication Data

Barnes, Emilie.
    [Minute meditations for women]
    Meet me where I am, Lord / Emilie Barnes.
        p. cm.
    Originally published: Minute meditations for women. Eugene, Or. : Harvest House Publishers, c1999.
    Includes bibliographical references (p.   ).

    ISBN-13: 978-0-7369-1332-4
    ISBN-10: 0-7369-1332-7

    1. Christian women—Prayer-books and devotions—English. I. Title.
BV4844.B36   2006
242'.643—dc22   2006003633

Printed in the United States of America

07   08   09   10   11   12   13 / BP-MS / 10   9   8   7   6   5   4   3

As a young woman in my thirties, I felt I had no skills. I'd been a full-time homemaker and done it well. However, with only a high school diploma, what could I possibly do after my children were out of the nest? Then God brought into my life a mentor Bible teacher, an upholder, an example, an exhorter, and a talented "you can do it" blessing—Florence Littauer. I dedicate this book to my very special friend and mentor. Florence has mentored me for over 35 years. She introduced me and Bob to my publisher, Harvest House, who has published all of our books since 1982.

My deepest thanks to Florence and Harvest House. They have encouraged me with every step I take.

God has gifted them as He has me and many of you who can do whatever your heart leads you to do.

Thank you to all those who have held my hand through my writing walk.

Emilie Barnes

Foreword

These devotions will encourage and challenge all aspects of your life including yourself, husbands, children, friends, and theology. I pray that some will make you laugh and some will even make you cry. As with all my books, I have made each devotion very practical and very readable. My desire is for you to know God in a more personal way.

Each of you will find your own time of day and individual location to spend time with these thoughts. In whatever situation you are in, I will be there with you.

I have placed three boxes in the top portion of each devotion so you can check off each devotion after you've read it. This way you can keep track of what you've read. This system also gives you the freedom to choose devotions that fit your need for that day.

Each brief entry carries a nugget of truth. You may say your own prayers or you can use mine to close your study. Try to carry through on the *Action* section of each reading. Become a doer of God's Word and not just a hearer. The *Reflection* section is for you to make a few personal notes of how you have been touched. This section can act as a journal for each reading.

May God richly bless your life as you enter into a daily walk with Him.

The Name of God

And to Seth, to him also a son was born;
and he called his name Enosh. Then men began
to call upon the name of the LORD.

—GENESIS 4:26

hroughout the book of Genesis, God uses different names for Himself to reveal certain aspects of His character. These names are especially important to a people with no written record of God's words and deeds. The character of God becomes clearer as He reveals His names, which include:

- Yahweh: Lord (Genesis 4:26)
- Yahweh Yir'eh: The Lord will provide (22:14)
- El Roi: The God who sees (16:13)

God is often known by the people who worship Him; for example, to Jacob He is "the God of my grandfather Abraham, or the awe-inspiring God of my father, Isaac" (31:42 NLT).

The way God has made Himself known to others enriches the depth and richness of our worship today. When we better understand the nature of God through His various names and what they mean, we can begin to

7

grasp the vastness of who God is. He certainly has depth and breadth of character. He is to be looked at in awe. The glorious radiance of His face does not permit us to look upon Him directly.

When people say that when they get to heaven they're going to ask God so and so, I stand in amazement that they don't seem to know who God really is. Truly God is an awesome God.

Prayer   Father God, as I look upon Your majesty through Your various names, I begin to grasp Your awesomeness. My limited mind prevents me from realizing how big You are. You are certainly an awe-inspiring God. I praise Your name always. Amen.

Action   Read over the list of the names of God and appreciate His awesome character.

Reflections

Thank You, God, for quiet places far from life's crowded ways, where our hearts find true contentment and our souls fill up with praise.

—AUTHOR UNKNOWN

The Names of God

Elohim . . . . CREATOR

El 'Elyon . . . . SOVEREIGN

El Shaddai . . . . GOD ALMIGHTY

Adonai . . . . LORD

Jehovah . . . . I AM

Jehovah Jireh . . . . PROVIDER

Jehovah Rapha . . . . HEALER

Jehovah Nissi . . . . THE LORD MY BANNER

Jehovah M'Kaddesh Kim . . . . SANCTIFIER

Jehovah Sabaoth . . . . LORD OF HOSTS

Jehovah Shalom . . . . PEACE

Jehovah Tsidkenu . . . . RIGHTEOUSNESS

Jehovah Shammah . . . . THE LORD IS THERE

Jehovah Raah . . . . SHEPHERD

Daily Blessing and Grace

❧ ❧ ❧

Incoporating the principle of Ephesians 5:21, we are to be submissive to one another. Run an errand, do something for your mate without being asked, give small gifts, give a compliment when appropriate, be willing to say "I'm sorry."

—AUTHOR UNKNOWN

This Sickness Is Not unto Death!

*This sickness is not unto death, but for the glory of God,
that the Son of God may be glorified by it.*

—JOHN 11:4

I have been under doctors' care for the last two-and-a-half years. I had every kind of test but my energy level was getting lower and lower, my weight was reduced by 30 pounds, and the travel and speaking I do was taking its toll. I was going to a very prominent oncologist for a second opinion in Newport Beach, California—a man who has had great success with making cancer patients well. He, too, ran his own series of tests, plus looking at all the notes from my previous doctors of the last few years. The day I was to meet him with his diagnosis for my illness, I was well surrounded by my Bob, our son, Brad, and our daughter, Jenny. As the doctor entered into the examining room he expressed great concern about the treatment I had been receiving. He was very upset that the last nine months had been wasted with no one aggressively making decisions on my behalf.

He stated that I had M.A.L.T. Cell Lymphoma, and I needed to start chemotherapy immediately. I was extremely anemic and needed two pints of blood. He also said I needed to cancel all seminars through the rest of the year if I was going to be his patient. Naturally we said, "Yes, yes, yes!" At last we found a doctor who was proactive and wanted to make me well. After our consultation I claimed John 11:4 as my sickness verse...may God be glorified through this whole process.

Prayer   *Father God, thank You for medical doctors and answered prayers. I appreciate so much the prayer warriors all across this country who pray for me daily. May your Son, Jesus, be glorified by this miracle. Amen.*

Action   Call a friend who is sick and let him or her know you are praying for good health. (Make the call brief.)

Reflections

□ □ □

The Flat Tire Wasn't a Fluke

*And we know that God causes all things
to work together for good to those who love God,
to those who are called according to His purpose.*

—ROMANS 8:28

What a great promise this is to the believer. For many years I thought that this passage was for everyone; however, I soon learned that with every promise there is a condition. The condition for this promise is found in the second half of that verse:

- to those who love God
- to those called according to His purpose

Make sure that your life meets these two qualifications before you lay claim to this promise.

God's mercy and healing power are beautifully illustrated in this story:

> Peter was riding his bicycle Sunday morning when the tire went flat. He examined it and knew that he couldn't repair it with a spare tube like he usually did. He had not run over anything, so this

13

tire failure was a fluke, and he would have to walk home. Not wanting to lose his only opportunity for a work-out, he decided to run his bike home as fast as he could.

When Peter got home he and his wife, Anna, discovered that their one-year-old son, Christian, had wandered over to the pool. They found him floating face down and unconscious. Horrified, they thought, "Lord, not another one."

On February 9, 1996, Peter and Anna had lost their six-year-old son, Andrew, to cancer. It was the greatest trial of their lives, yet the Lord gave them the strength and grace they needed to trust in Him. They later used their experience to minister to others. Chris and Lisa, a couple whose son Anthony has been battling with cancer, say that they would have been lost without the gentle ministry of support from Peter and Anna.

Later that day, the hospital waiting room was filled with praying Christian friends and family members. Everyone from the home study that Peter and Anna attended were there, with the exception of one guy who was working that day, but even he had called in to pray. The family of God was at its best, supporting and praying for this family in time of need.

Little one-year-old Christian is fine. The neurologists said they think he was in the water no more than two minutes and had suffered no permanent brain damage. Today he is running around, doing one-year-old things, and Peter and Anna, as well as the whole home-study group, are looking up, praising God.[1]

Prayer   *Father God, after looking back over almost 45 years as a believer, I can honestly testify that all things that have crossed my life have worked toward the good. You have always revealed the truth for every happening. Thank You for sharing so much of Your love through the events in my walk with You. Amen.*

Action   Write down several happenings in your life. Beside each one, state what good came about in your life as a result.

Reflections

---

*I know Christ dwells within me all the
time, guiding me and inspiring me
whenever I do or say anything.
A light of which I caught
no glimmer before comes to
me at the very moment
when it is needed.*

—SAINT THERESE OF LISIEUX

I love you today, where you are and as you are. You do not have to be anything but what you are for me to love you. I love you now; not sometime when you are worthy, but today when you may need love most.

❧ ❧ ❧

I will not withold my love or withdraw it. There are no strings on my love, no price. I will not force it upon you when you are not ready. It is just there, freely offered with both hands.

❧ ❧ ❧

Take what you want today. The more you take, the more there is. It is good if you can return love; but if you cannot today, that is all right too. Love is its own joy. Bless me by letting me love you today.

—AUTHOR UNKNOWN

Happy Husband's Help

Let all be harmonious, sympathetic, brotherly,
kindhearted, and humble in spirit....You were called for
the very purpose that you might inherit a blessing.

—1 PETER 3:8,9

Afew years ago Bob and I were in Charleston, South Carolina, touring an old African-American craft district when we ran across an apron that had "If Mama Ain't Happy, No One Is Happy" embroidered on it. We realized that the maker of this apron had captured the essence of marriage. In a healthy marriage both partners are happy in the roles they play. When a spouse is happy and feels appreciated, he or she will want to be of help to the other. If your mate is unhappy, the last thing he wants to do is help you out or please you.

I certainly recognize and acknowledge that you are not responsible for your husband's happiness; he alone must be accountable for that. However, we as wives do play a large part in making our mates feel appreciated. Don't take it for granted that he is thoroughly aware that he is appreciated. As a marriage partner, it's important that you take the time to show and say verbally that your mate is appreciated for all he does for the family. In most cases his boss at work gives little praise for his efforts, so your family's praises might be the only positive affirmations he receives each day. As marriage partners, we want to treat our spouses as well as we do our close friends.

Bob and I genuinely want to share our appreciation for each other. We never want to take anything for granted. We often say, "Just another way to show that I love you" before we do a courteous act to or for each other. A little "thank you" goes a long way to show our mates that their acts of efforts are appreciated. Make today a new beginning of loving and caring and serving in your marriage.

Prayer   *Father God, from the bottom of my heart I want my husband to know that he is appreciated and loved. I want to show him how much I like the things he does for me and our family. Let today be a new day in our lives. May I be willing to treat him like a king, so he can treat me like a queen. Amen.*

Action   Express your gratitude and appreciation to your husband by saying "thank you" for specific areas.

Reflections

Relief and Restoration

Come to me, all you who are weary and burdened, and I will give you rest. Take my yoke upon you and learn from me, for I am gentle and humble in heart, and you will find rest for your souls.

—MATTHEW 11:28-29

Back in the days when I had a little more time and a lot less money, I enjoyed the process of restoring old, beat-up furniture and decorative items. With a little paint or varnish, a yard or two of fabric, and a little creative imagination, almost any worn-out item could be restored to beauty or usefulness. I used to find such joy in this activity.

Now when I feel broken and worn, I wonder if my heavenly Father finds the same kind of joy in restoring me. For restoration is exactly what He promises us through Scripture.

"He restores my soul," sings the psalmist.

"The God of all grace, who called you to His eternal glory in Christ, will Himself perfect, confirm, strengthen and establish you," says Peter.

In the Old Testament, God repeatedly promised His people through the prophets that He would restore the health of their nation.

Jesus, throughout His earthly ministry, restored physical health, spiritual health, even physical life...and passed that restorative power on to His followers through the Holy Spirit.

Even the biblical depictions of the end times are a magnificent epic of restoration, a promise to bring about a new heaven and a new earth—all fixed, redeemed, and shining as good as new.

Magnificently "all better."

And that, of course, is what we all long for, especially in the rainy seasons of our lives.

When illness strikes, when experiences knock us low, when life leaves us wounded, our natural heart-cry to our heavenly Father is the cry of a child: "Please make it better."

And He does just that. I believe it with all my heart. How does He do it? As I see it, God has several favorite methods.

Every one of us has benefited from the normal healing processes built into creation. And these natural processes are truly miraculous. I am astonished to see the ways that cells can regenerate to close a wound, knit a broken bone together, or combat an infection. I'm amazed at the way the human mind can adapt and move forward after a disappointment or even a crushing tragedy. I am astounded by the resilience of the human spirit, the way people can rebound from a setback to live creative and positive lives.

Healing is built into the very design of the world.

I believe God also works through human beings to do His restorative work. Traditional and alternative doctors can be agents of remarkable healing, and so can ministers and therapists and counselors, and all those with the spiritual gift of healing. And so can loving friends who pour their energies in prayer and practical help.

And I truly believe that when it suits His purposes, God intervenes directly in the natural processes He originally set in motion. I know of too many instances—either those I have directly witnessed or those told to me by people I trust—of miraculous, instantaneous healings of mind and body and spirit. And yet I have to remember it doesn't always happen that way. Not everyone is healed suddenly. Not everyone is even healed in a physical sense.

Restoration is not always instantaneous.

Unfortunately, sickness and brokenness and death are also part of life. But God is God. Our loving, redemptive, restorative Father retains the perogative of being in charge of all things, which means that His restoration proceeds on His timetable and according to His priorities.

By the Lord's mercy we are being healed, being made perfect in a process that will take our entire lifetimes...and perhaps even longer...to complete. We can feel the gentle touch of God's comfort, soft as a mother's kiss, the quiet reminder that He is still here. That calms us and keeps us going.

God brings beauty out of brokenness and gently guides His children into wholeness and maturity. How can we not trust Him to finish the job in us?

Healing is intended to be a partnership. God does the restoration, but we are not passive. We are expected to respond and participate in the process by following God's plan for our lives and keep our hearts open to Him, learning more about how He works, and offering Him our hearts. We need to stay close to God by reading the Scriptures, spending time in prayer, listening to His Word about what our part is in our healing. And, most importantly, we need to obey Him.

Here on earth, the restoration we experience is an ongoing process, truly miraculous but partial and problematic. Here on earth the very process of healing leaves us marked and scarred (not to mention wrinkled and sagging). In the end, though, the healing we are promised is whole and complete. When God is through with us, we will be more real than we ever thought possible—as well as unscarred and unwrinkled and energetic and full of life and love.

I don't know about you, but I just can't wait!

Prayer   *Father God, thank You for Your healing touch.*
You restore my soul to gladness. You give me
rest in the midst of my trials and provide relief
from my burdens. You are an amazing God, and
I love You. Amen.

Action   Reach out to someone who is hurting and
feeling stressed. Let her know you care.
Share your own struggles and the God of
comfort so she will know she's not alone.

Reflections

A Record Mile Run

*I can do all things through Him who
strengthens me.*

—Philippians 4:13

One evening my grandson, Chad, who was in the sixth grade, called and wanted to know which verse of Scripture said that a person could do all things. After thinking for a few moments this passage came to mind. I asked Chad why he needed to know. He replied that tomorrow he was running the mile for the Presidential Physical Fitness Certificate, and he was really nervous about this event. He said his stomach was churning, and he wasn't going to be able to sleep, which would cause him to be tired tomorrow. He was worried that he wouldn't do well.

He wanted to read this verse so he could be at ease and do a good job in the race. We talked for a while. I had a word of prayer with him and hung up the phone. The next morning I called to see how he slept, and he assured me he was good and rested. He also said his mom had prepared him a high-energy breakfast. He was off to school with confidence that he would do his very best.

That afternoon at about three-thirty the phone rang and Chad was on the other end with a cheerful voice that stated, "Grammy, I won the race in record time. I know that the verse and your prayers really helped me. I will always remember that verse when I need reassurance. Thanks, Grammy."

What a thrill for me to realize that a 12-year-old boy went to Scripture to help him in life.

Prayer   Father God, I do know that I can do all things through Christ. He is my strength and my assurance. He helps me when things are tough. Thank You. Amen.

Action   Claim Philippians 4:13 when you need encouragement.

Reflections

It takes so little to make us glad,
Just a cheering clasp of a friendly hand,
Just a word from one who can understand;
And we finish the task we long had planned,
And we lose the doubt and the fear we had—
So little it takes to make us glad.

—IDA GOLDSMITH MORRIS

□ □ □

Finding Complete Happiness

*Enter His gates with thanksgiving,
and His courts with praise. Give thanks to Him;
bless His name.*

—PSALM 100:4

I f only I could take a shopping cart to K-Mart and Wal-Mart and shop until I had all the stuff I wanted—then I would be happy!" Have you echoed that thought before? I had a very close friend who often verbalized, "If only I could have a bigger house, a bigger car, a bigger ring, live in a certain city—then I would be happy." After 25 years she is still looking for happiness in possessions. How sad to watch her downward spiral into depression because she's always looking for happiness in the wrong places.

The Scriptures are quite clear that a thankful heart is a happy heart. To have complete happiness we must enter into the Lord's presence with thanksgiving. I have found in my own life that when I am appreciative for all I have, my mental, physical, and spiritual dimensions are at balance with each other. The family chores run smoother and the mood of my home is more relaxed. I'm excited to bounce out of bed each day challenged by what may come

25

my way. During this time of peace and tranquility my friends seem to bond closer to me. I'm fun to be around. There is an air of positiveness that is transmitted from my presence.

People like to be around people who are positive and edifying. We build up instead of tear down. A smile and laughter is ever-present on my face.

We need to take our eyes off of stuff and become women of thanksgiving. When we are thankful, the possessions will be in proper perspective and happiness will not elude us.

Prayer   Father God, take away my focus on acquiring things. Let me be a person with a thankful heart. I know my happiness does not depend upon me acquiring possessions. Help me break away from this materialism. I do thank You for all I have. Amen.

Action   Take time tonight around the dinner table to express thanks for all that God has given you and your family. And remember the little things, too.

Reflections

□ □ □

Be Willing to Say "Thank You!"

Love is patient, love is kind, and is not jealous;
love does not brag and is not arrogant.

—1 CORINTHIANS 13:4

As fellow believers, we must be sensitive to the fact that we don't want to take our spouses for granted. After 43 years of marriage, my Bob and I continue to work on this area of our life. We continue to do little courtesies for each other. He is such a gracious gentleman wherever we go. Women often comment to me what a warm, soft, and tender man he is. He still opens my car door and lets me enter buildings first. He brings me flowers and takes me to special shows. He asks me rather than tells me, considers me equal to him, and is willing to seek and hear my opinion. He is always ready to say thank you.

Likewise, I'm continually extending my appreciation to my Bob. I never want to be void of my thankfulness for him as my husband.

Taking a mate for granted is one of the main reasons our country experiences a 50-percent divorce rate, with a higher percentage for second and third marriages. Don't

27

get caught in the trap of expecting your mate to do so-and-so just because he is your spouse.

As the years fly by, Bob and I continually discuss our feelings toward each other. Are we still filling each other's "emotional tanks," or are we drifting into complacency?

Appreciation is your choosing; choose today to stop taking your spouse for granted. Get excited about life and its many challenges. Choose to be grateful and to express your appreciation. The more you do, the easier it becomes. You will have a fuller and richer life when you focus on thankfulness.

Prayer   *Father God, don't let me become complacent about my mate. I want to always be an encourager. Thank You for giving me a husband who affirms me as a woman. He plays a large part in helping me develop into the woman You want me to become. Amen.*

Action   Tonight tell your husband how much you appreciate him. Make his favorite dessert.

Reflections

□ □ □

What You Can't Do Can Be Fun

A faithful [woman] will abound with blessings.

—PROVERBS 28:20

ave you ever met people with limited income who are rich and rich people who are poor? I certainly have, and I love to see how different people stretch their money to become wealthy. I have a very good friend who can make a purse out of a sow's ear. She just knows how to shop. She lives in a very affluent area of Southern California, so she takes great delight in going into second-time-around stores to purchase very nice clothing at greatly reduced prices. Another friend has made her rental condo into a dollhouse. She takes old furniture and gives it the latest artistic touch, and she adds a few touches with fabric accents that she makes on her sewing machine. My Bob used to have a barber whose wife loved to drive a Lincoln Town Car, but they couldn't afford one on his income. They would watch the ads and rent one for the weekend. That was just enough to satisfy her need for wanting to drive a large car.

Another couple I know love to camp along the California coastline. For very little cost they will visit a different state park each year and have a wonderful time with their family. They—and you—can find happiness within a budget.

Don't spend time thinking about what you don't have, but count your blessings for the things you do have. Don't wait until the next big raise to do something bigger than you are used to. Instead, find happiness where you are. Make the best and most of what you have. One way to minimize the stress over a tight budget is to make the decision to stop using a lack of funds to justify your unhappiness. This isn't an "if only I had" world. Enjoy what you have as much as possible.

Prayer Father God, You have given me more than I could ever thank You for. As a young girl I never thought I would be so blessed. Let me continue to enjoy what I can't do, and let me shout "thank You" for what I have. Amen.

Action Do something fun this weekend that costs little or no money.

Reflections

□ □ □

Home Robbers

*And the worries of the world, and the deceitfulness
of riches, and the desires for other things enter
in and choke the word, and it
becomes unfruitful.*

—MARK 4:19

*I*f we're not on guard, the things of the world will enter into our homes and rob us of contentment. We get trapped in: "We need this"; "we don't have enough of that"; "if only my kitchen was bigger"; "my dishes are so old"; "I don't have the right wallpaper"; "the cupboards need a fresh coat of paint"; "I can't entertain until I have new carpet"; and so on. Do these joy-robbing phrases sound familiar? Have you uttered a few of them?

I encourage you to take a moment to be refreshed. Instead of focusing on a home beautiful, contemplate a home filled with the spirit of loveliness—the spirit of warmth and caring. I talk with hundreds of women like you who truly have a heart for home. Your situation may be unusual, but like most women you probably want to be a home builder not a home robber.

Do you long for a home that is warm and welcoming, comfortable and freeing? A place where you can express the uniqueness of your God-given talents and nurture

31

your relationships with people you love? Do you desire a home that reflects your personality and renews your soul—a place that glows with a spirit of loveliness? I believe this spirit is already in your heart. You *can* stop the home robbers at the curb and not give them entrance to your home.

No matter how little or how much you have, you can experience the results of having a godly home. Take steps toward making your home a sanctuary—a place of security, trust, and comfort. A place to reenergize, pray, and dream. You can begin with a friendly welcome at the front door for your family and friends.

Prayer
Father God, there are so many people who want to steal the joy of my home. Cast away those acquaintances who are negative in thought. I want to cherish my family and friends who build up my desire to reflect Your spirit of loveliness in my home. Amen.

Action
Sweep down, scrub down, hose down the front entrance to your home. Purchase a sign, a flag, or a plaque that tells those coming in that they are welcome.

Reflections

One-by-One

There is an appointed time for everything.
And there is a time for every
event under heaven.

—ECCLESIASTES 3:1

In one of the old *McGuffey Readers* there is a story about a clock that had been running for a long, long time on the mantelpiece. One day the clock began to think about how many times during the year ahead it would have to tick. It counted up the seconds: 31,536,000 in one year. The old clock just got too tired and said, "I can't do it." It stopped right there. When somebody reminded the clock that it didn't have to tick the 31,536,000 seconds all at one time, but rather one-by-one, it began to run again and everything was all right.

God has given us an eternal perspective so that we can look beyond the routines of life. Nevertheless, God has not revealed all of life's mysteries. In Ecclesiastes 3:11, Solomon writes, "[God] has made everything appropriate in its time. He has also set eternity in their heart, yet so that man will not find out the work which God has done from the beginning even to the end."

As I get older, I sometimes get out of bed early in the morning and see what a long day lies ahead of me. So many things to do: appointments to keep, hours on the phone, preparations of at least three meals, giving quality time to my family, clothes to wash, clothes to iron—and on and on it goes. On many days it will be 16 or 18 hours before I can turn back the sheets and crawl into the cozies of my blankets. To be honest, there are days I want to forget it all and crawl back into bed, but a small voice inside of me says, "Emilie, you don't have to do it all at once. Just put your feet on the floor and take the first step of the day." When I'm able to break up the large segment into small pieces I can stop being overwhelmed and do a little at a time. What's so amazing is that I can do everything I had on my list—and I can even laugh along the way. A long journey begins with the first step.

Prayer   *Father God, thank You for letting me see the whole picture and to realize it doesn't have to be accomplished at one time. I appreciate seeing each little segment. Thanks for each new beginning. Amen.*

Action   When you wake up, what is the first thing you need to do? Do it. What is the second thing you need to do? Do it. Take your day one step at a time.

Reflections

Be Glad You Have Problems

We also exult in our tribulations, knowing that tribulation brings about perseverance; and perseverance, proven character; and proven character, hope;—and hope, does not disappoint.

—ROMANS 5:3

*M*e? Have problems? I don't think so. In fact, I wake up each morning trying to eliminate all the problems I encounter. It's hard for my human side to see any good that might come from problems. They take so much time to solve, and I often get depressed during the process. No, no good can come from having problems...

Think again because God says that problems are given to us to strengthen our Christian walk. Norman Vincent Peale once said:

> So be glad—yes, actually *be glad* that you have problems. Be grateful for them as implying that God has confidence in your ability to handle these problems with which He has entrusted you. Adopt this attitude toward problems and it will tend to siphon off the depression you may have

developed from negative reactions to them. And as you develop the habit of thinking in hopeful terms about your problems, you will find yourself doing much better with them.

This will add to your enjoyment of life too, for one of the few greatest satisfactions of this life is to handle problems efficiently and well. Moreover, this successful handling tends to build up your faith that, through God's help and guidance, you have what it takes to deal with anything that may ever face you.[2]

Peale has made a few excellent observations that show me that my faith grows during troubled times. Problems do seem to make me more humble and more appreciative of what God is trying to accomplish in my life. "Okay God, I see what You are attempting to do when You give me problems, but could You start out slowly? I really don't want to become a spiritual giant too quickly."

Prayer   *Father God, thanks for loving me enough to give me problems. Also, Your confidence that I can handle them reassures me that I can do it. Please give me the insights so that I can work through them in a way that would be pleasing to You. Amen.*

Action   List three problems that you currently have. Under each statement write what you think God is trying to teach you through these situations.

Reflections

Become One Another

*So we, who are many, are one body in Christ,
and individually members one of another.*

—ROMANS 12:5

n Scripture we often hear the terms *one spirit, one belief, one life,* and *one another.* That's when we begin to realize that God wants us to grow in oneness. Togetherness helps bond our relationship with God. Early in the book of Genesis we read, "For this cause a man shall leave his father and his mother, and shall cleave to his wife; and they shall become one flesh" (2:24).

When we join forces with others we become stronger, and it becomes difficult to weaken our positions. There is great strength in unity. This concept is at the center of why we need to be in a church that's teaching God's Word every time we meet. We need the support of others if we are to grow in Christ. Today I want you to examine various Scriptures to impress upon you the importance of oneness:

Romans 12:5:	belong to one another
12:10:	be devoted to one another
12:10:	honor one another
12:18:	live in harmony with one another

Prayer   *Father God, let me realize how important it is to have a support system of fellow believers who have kindred spirits. I cannot walk the journey alone—I need friends who will encourage me and lift me up. I am not an island unto myself. Amen.*

Action   Use today's Scripture and the "One-Another" Scriptures for the next few days. Look these passages up in your Bible and meditate on them.

Reflections

Lord, make me an instrument of your peace.
Where there is hatred, let me sow love;
Where there is injury, pardon;
Where there is doubt, faith;
Where there is despair, hope;
Where there is darkness, light;
and where there is sadness, joy.

—ST. FRANCIS OF ASSISI

"One-Another" Teachings in the New Testament

Romans 12:18 Live at peace with one another*

Accept one another

1 Corinthians 1:10 Agree with one another

10:24 Look out for one another*

16:20 Greet one another with a holy kiss

Galatians 5:13 Serve one another

6:1 Carry one another's burdens*

Ephesians 4:2 Bear with one another*

4:32 Be kind to one another

4:32 Be compassionate to one another

4:32 Forgive one another

5:19 Speak to one another with psalms, hymns, and spiritual songs

5:21 Submit to one another

Colossians 3:13 Bear with one another*

3:13 Forgive one another

3:16 Teach one another

1 Thessalonians 4:9 Love one another*

5:11 Encourage one another

5:11 Build up one another*

5:13 Live in peace with one another*

5:15 Be kind to one another*

Hebrews 10:24 Spur on one another

10:25 Meet with one another

13:1 Love one another*

James 5:16 Confess your sins to one another*

5:16 Pray for one another*

1 Peter 1:22 Love one another

3:8 Live in harmony with one another

4:9 Offer hospitality to one another

5:14 Greet one another with a kiss of love

1 John 1:7 Have fellowship with one another

3:11 Love one another

3:16 Lay down your lives for one another*

3:23 Love one another

4:7 Love one another

2 John 5 Love one another

* These statements have been changed from "each other" to "one another"

Giving and gratitude go together like humor and laughter, like having one's back rubbed and the sigh that follows, like a blowing wind and the murmur of wind chimes. Gratitude keeps alive the rhythm of grace given and grace grateful, a lively lilt that lightens a heavy world.

—LEWIS B. SMEDES

What Must I Do?

Sirs, what must I do to be saved?

—ACTS 16:30

hat must I do to be saved?" asked the Philippian jailer. "Believe in the Lord Jesus" was Paul and Silas' answer. This one question and one answer summarize the teachings of the New Testament. It's not too complicated; it's very basic. From pastors, to doctors, to financial investors, to mothers and fathers, "What must I do?" is one of the most common questions around.

Jesus tells us that He came to earth that we might have life and have it more abundantly (John 10:10). How do we achieve an abundant Christian life? First, we believe with a faith so strong that the storms of life can threaten, but they cannot destroy. The abundant life begins for us on earth and, in a natural transition, leads us into eternity. Our faith grows as we learn.

A wise man once expressed his observation of people over the years: "Most folks are just about as happy as they set out to be." My Bob and I also confirm that observation of life. People do what they want to do. May you answer the question "What must I do?" with the same confidence the disciples had when they said, "Believe in the Lord Jesus, and you shall be saved" (Acts 16:31).

If you have never answered this common question of life, respond positively today. Before the sun sets confirm in your heart that you are a child of God.

If you take these steps, you can know *without a doubt* that you are a Christian:

1. Admit your spiritual need. Acknowledge to yourself and to God the truth set forth in Romans 3:23—you are a sinner.

2. Repent. Turn from your sin and, with God's help, start living in a way that pleases Him (1 John 1:9).

3. Believe that Jesus Christ died for you on the cross and rose again (Acts 16:30-31).

4. Receive, through prayer, Jesus Christ into your heart and life (John 3:16; 14:13,14). Let the following be a model for you:

    Dear Lord Jesus, I know I am a sinner....I believe You died for my sins and then rose from the grave. Right now I turn from my sins and open the door of my heart and life to You. I receive You as my personal Lord and Savior. Thank You for saving me. Amen.

5. Tell a believing friend and a pastor about your commitment to the Lord (Matthew 28:19,20).

Whether you just now received Jesus as your Lord and Savior or you did so decades ago, you are one of God's precious children. You need not wonder about your place in His family. You're in for life—and for eternal life.

Prayer   *Father God, I want You to guide my life. Help me grow in the knowledge You have given me through the Scriptures. Lead me to a church that will teach me all about You. Amen.*

Action   Accept Jesus as your personal Savior today. If you have a Bible, write on the title page the month, day, and year of this decision.

Reflections

Marriage is not just spiritual communion and passionate embraces; marriage is also three-meals-a-day and remembering to carry the garbage out.

—JOYCE BROTHERS

God helps us to do what we can,
and endure what we must,
even in the darkest hours.
But more, He wants to teach us
that there are no rainbows without
storm clouds and there
are no diamonds without heavy
pressure and enormous heat.

—AUTHOR UNKNOWN

Give of Yourself

Give, and it will be given to you; good measure,
pressed down, shaken together, running over,
they will pour into your lap. For by your standard of
measure it will be measured to you in return.

—LUKE 6:38

Lord, make me a channel of thy peace
That where there is hatred I bring love,
That where there is discord I may bring
harmony,
That where there is error I may bring truth,
That where there is doubt I may bring faith,
That where there is despair I may bring hope,
That where there are shadows I may bring thy light,
That where there is sadness I may bring joy.

Lord, grant that I may seek rather
to comfort—than to be comforted;
To understand—than to be understood;
To love—than to be loved;
For it is by giving that one receives
It is by self-forgetting that one finds;
It is by forgiving that one is forgiven;
It is by dying that one awakens to eternal life.[3]

—*St. Francis of Assisi*

The world waits until someone gives before giving back; however, Scripture tells us to give first then it will be added unto you. Are you waiting for someone to give to you before you are willing to give to him or her? If it's not working, try the reverse: Give to that person first.

Prayer   Father God, You are truly a God of giving. Thank You so much for all You have given me. I can never repay You for all Your graciousness. Amen.

Action   Step out today in faith and give.

Reflections

Conduct is what we do; character
is what we are. Conduct is the
outward life; character is the
life unseen, hidden within, yet
evidenced by that which is seen....
Character is the state of the heart;
conduct is its outward expression.
Character is the root of the tree,
conduct, the fruit it bears.

—E.M. BOUNDS

A Heart Fully Devoted

*When the time of mourning was over, David sent and
brought her to his house and she became his wife; then she
bore him a son. But the thing that David had done was
evil in the sight of the LORD.*

—2 SAMUEL 11:27

*D*avid, despite his unique knowledge and experience of God,
apparently did not foresee any
grave complications when he committed adultery
with Bathsheba. As king he was accustomed to getting
what he wanted, and he wanted Bathsheba. But to
keep his disobedience to God from being revealed,
David finally ordered the death of Uriah, Bathsheba's
husband.

The lie we tell may seem an isolated instance.
But often we end up having to deny we lied, digging
ourselves deeper into a hole. We can even begin impli-
cating others, asking them to lie for us.

If people will steal, they will not balk at lying; it
is foolish to look for honor among thieves. A woman
who cheats on her husband will not be a trustworthy
friend either. We do, indeed, weave "a tangled web"
when we first decide to deceive.

King David stands as a prime example not only of
sin but also of the reality of forgiveness. The betrayals

of godly character seem too numerous to count; the sordid story would seem surely to constitute the end of David's glory.

But what is God's final opinion of David? Years after David's death, God said of him, his heart was "fully devoted to the Lord his God" (1 Kings 11:4). What an epitaph! How could this be after all of David's sins?

The answer lies in Psalm 51, David's prayer of repentance.

David's story proves that our sins, no matter how repugnant, need not separate us permanently from God and his plan for us. The path back to him lies in the complete repentance mirrored in Psalm 51. The restoration to fellowship with God results not from a halfhearted "forgive me," but a broken spirit.

God specializes in miracle cures, and we, as well as David, can be known as those fully devoted to the Lord our God, no matter how serious our character lapses, or sins, may be. God knows how to make clean hearts out of dirty ones. Praise him![4]

—*Barbara Bush*

The history of the Christian church is full of biographies of men and women who have fallen into sin and have not been separated permanently from God and His plan. No matter where we are in our walk with God, we need not be separated from God. He will restore us back to the fold if we respond with a broken spirit.

May God reach down and lift all those who have slipped in their walk with Him. David's fall should put on guard all who have not fallen and save from despair all those who have fallen.

Prayer Father God, today is a reminder that when a person takes his or her eyes off You and, instead, focuses on personal lusts, the result is spiritual separation from You. Help us remember what can happen when we lose sight of Your calling for our lives. Thank You also for lifting up and restoring those who have fallen. Amen.

Action Read Psalm 51.

Reflections

Only when you're studying and applying God's truth in the Bible can you discern what's right or wrong, true or false, loving or cruel, profitable or foolish, noble or cowardly.

---

*[O Lord,] for the sacrifice of Jesus Christ
offered upon the cross for me; for his sake,
ease me of the burden of my sins, and give
me grace that by the call of the Gospel I
may rise from the slumber of sin into the
newness of life. Let me live according to
those holy rules which thou hast
this day prescribed in thy holy word;
make me to know what is acceptable
in thy holy word; make me to know what
is acceptable in thy sight, and therein
to delight, open the eyes of my
understanding, and help me thoroughly
to examine myself concerning my
knowledge, faith and repentance,
increase my faith, and direct me
to the true object Jesus Christ,
the way, the truth and the life.*

—GEORGE WASHINGTON

Give Us This Day

Our Father who art in heaven, hallowed be Thy name.
Thy kingdom come. Thy will be done, on earth as it is in heaven.
Give us this day our daily bread. And forgive us our debts, as
we also have forgiven our debtors. And do not lead us into
temptation, but deliver us from evil. For Thine is the kingdom,
and the power, and the glory, forever. Amen.

—MATTHEW 6:9-13

The "Lord's Prayer" is a model for our prayers. It begins with adoration of God (verse 9), acknowledges subjection to His will (verse 10), asks of Him (verses 11-13), and ends with an offering of praise (verse 13).

The fatherhood of God toward His children is the basis for Jesus' frequent teaching about prayer. "Your Father knows what you need," Jesus told His disciples, "before you ask him!" (Matthew 6:8). Jesus presents a pattern that the church has followed throughout the centuries.

Prayer begins by honoring the name of God. He is worthy of honor because He is the heavenly King, yet His rule is being extended over the earth as well. Because He is King, we can entrust all our physical needs to His

51

provision, asking Him to "give us our food for today," instead of worrying about the future.

Since God is our merciful Father, we also seek forgiveness from Him while we forgive those who have sinned against us. Finally, we ask our Father to keep us from yielding to temptation and to deliver us from the evil one, for our God is able to defeat any evil that comes against us.

This model of prayer is one that should be engraved upon our hearts—and the hearts of the children that God has given us. Information stored in our memory bank can't be taken from us. Trust the Lord each day for your provision.

Prayer   *Father God, Your model prayer has come to me in the night on several occasions and has given me great comfort. Your prayer has become my prayer, and I enjoy reciting it often when I think of You. Amen.*

Action   Memorize the Lord's Prayer.

Reflections

☐ ☐ ☐

You Don't Always Have to Win

*For the anger of man does not achieve the
righteousness of God.*

—JAMES 1:20

I don't know about you, but I have never won an argument. Even though my Bob might say, "I give, you win!" my heart feels heavy and certainly not victorious. It certainly doesn't feel like we've been drawn together. In fact, disagreements drive us farther apart. When disagreements arise, the interaction between the parties can be far from ideal.

An argument is when two or more parties are trying to prove their positions. Very seldom does anyone listen to learn anything; each party is trying to overpower his or her opponent with oratory or volume. Rarely do people feel good in this situation. There are usually feelings of resentment, anger, frustration, and stress.

However, if you allow someone else to win a disagreement, it's often the case that both of you are winners. It's often a very rewarding experience that allows your relationship to grow. When you let someone else win, you are showing that it's no big deal to always be right. I know this can be a difficult assignment because in our competitive society we are taught that winning is everything.

When you are willing to let someone else win, you will find yourself better able to listen because you aren't trying to overpower the other person with your persuasion.

Yes, there are some critical positions that must be defended, but those are usually few in life. These points must be defended because of your moral and biblical position.

Here are several key verses dealing with anger that help us understand the process outlined in Scripture:

- "A quick-tempered man acts foolishly" (Proverbs 14:17).

- "A gentle answer turns away wrath, but a harsh word stirs up anger" (Proverbs 15:1).

- "Let everyone be quick to hear, slow to speak and slow to anger" (James 1:19).

- "Do not let the sun go down on your anger" (Ephesians 4:26).

Prayer   *Father God, I appreciate that You have given me the ability to let someone else win an argument. It's okay not to always be right, and I don't feel any less a person because I also benefit. I don't have to "win" to be content. Amen.*

Action   In your next disagreement try this idea to see how it works. What were the benefits?

Reflections

The "I Can't" Club

*No temptation has overtaken you but such as is
common to man; and God is faithful, who will not allow
you to be tempted beyond what you are able, but with
the temptation will provide the way of escape also,
that you may be able to endure it.*

—1 CORINTHIANS 10:13

For thousands of years a popular club has been offering memberships throughout the world. It's a prolific club. It's the "I Can't" club.

Under the bylaws, club members are required to make "I can't" statements with conviction: "I can't help but hate after what he's done to me"; "I can't quit this sin"; "I can't forgive again!" Because of the fervor of these statements, it sounds as if each one is an unchangeable, universal law.

Everyone is subject to one law of science, the law of gravity—the force that pulls every object to the center of the earth. In a similar way, members of the "I Can't" club are prisoners to the downward pull of defeat—they are not only ground-bound, but sin-bound.

Do you feel bound to a specific sin? Does quitting the "I Can't" club seem impossible? The Father refuses to let "can't" be the universal password of his children. At your salvation he gave you the Spirit of God so that you would have the *strength* of God. He made it possible for you to overcome any sin. How? By replacing one law with another: The law of the Spirit of life set me free from the law of sin and death (Romans 8:2).

Let's think about the law of gravity again. Can you imagine a 190-ton mass of metal rising against gravity's pull? Impossible? It can't be done! Oh, yes it can...by using a "higher law." When you, in faith, give yourself over to the principle of aerodynamics, you can enter an airplane with full confidence that it will fly you from one city to another. You are no longer ground-bound.

Similarly, when you, in faith, give yourself over to the Spirit's control, the "I can't" statements will no longer bind you. When God fills your spirit with his Spirit and infuses you with his strength, you are no longer captive to any temptation. Every *can't* becomes a can.[5]

June Hunt, an award-winning author and host of a nationally proclaimed radio show "Hope for the Heart," has expressed how so many of us belong to the "I Can't" club, but through the salvation of Jesus we can escape from the prison-binding sins and be cut loose from them with a new freedom we have never before experienced. We can take our "I can'ts" and make them into "I cans." We have to decide who we will live for. We have to choose a life of confusion and doubt or a life of freedom and joy.

Today, take that way of escape. You'll change your whole attitude and gain eternal life.

Prayer   *Father God, 1 Corinthians 10:3 is a great verse of Scripture. What a freeing thought to know that all my sins are common to man and that* with each sin You have given me a way to escape so I will be able to endure it. Amen.

Action   Today claim that way of escape. Change your "can'ts" into "cans."

Reflections

Lord, this humble house we'd keep sweet with play and calm with sleep. Help us so that we may give beauty to the lives we live. Let Thy love and let Thy grace shine upon our dwelling place.

—EDGAR A. GUEST

I'm drinking from the saucer
If God gives me strength and courage,
When thy way grows steep and rough,
I'll not ask for any other blessings—
I'm already blessed enough.
May I never be too busy,
To help bear another's load.
I'm drinking from the saucer,
'Cause my cup has overflowed!

—AUTHOR UNKNOWN

□ □ □

Is Your Glass Half-Full?

And God saw all that He had made, and behold,
it was very good. And there was evening and there
was morning, the sixth day.

—GENESIS 1:31

As we look at life are we bound to the idea that bad things happen to people? Look at all the bad news on television and radio. The newspapers are full of disasters: people dying of illness, accidents, drownings, fires destroying property, uprisings in third-world countries, and on and on. Do you sometimes ask God, "Why me?"

As we look around, we get the idea that everything is falling apart, and our whole world is in a spiral downward. Charles L. Allen expressed himself toward this idea through our perspective: our glasses aren't half-empty, but they are really half-full. He says, "It seems to be a general belief that the will of God is to make things distasteful for us, like taking medicine when we are sick or going to the dentist. Somebody needs to tell us that sunrise is also God's will. In fact, the good things in life far outweigh the bad. There are more sunrises than cyclones."

His glass was certainly half-full.

There's a story of a young boy who was on top of a pile of horse manure digging as fast and as hard as he could. His father, seeing his son work so hard on a pile of smelly waste, asked, "Weston, what are you doing on that pile of horse manure?" Weston replied, "Daddy, with this much horse manure there must be a pony here somewhere." This son certainly had his glass half-full. You, too, can choose to be positive in all events of life. There is goodness in everything—if we will only look for it.

Prayer   *Father God, thank You for helping me be a positive person. I appreciate You giving me the ability to be an encourager to those around me. It certainly makes life so much more exciting. Amen.*

Action   Take any situation that comes and find the goodness therein. Look at the sunset and praise God for its beauty.

Reflections

Not by Bread Alone

*And He humbled you and let you be hungry, and fed you
with manna which you did not know, nor did your fathers know,
that He might make you understand that man does not live
by bread alone, but man lives by everything that proceeds
out of the mouth of the LORD.*

—DEUTERONOMY 8:3

an does not live by bread alone,
but by beauty and harmony,
truth and goodness, work and
recreation, affection and friendship, aspiration and
worship.

Not by bread alone, but by the splendor of
the firmament at night, the glory of the heavens at
dawn, the blending of colors at sunset, the loveliness of magnolia trees, the magnificence of mountains.

Not by bread alone, but by the majesty of ocean
breakers, the shimmer of moonlight on a calm
lake, the flashing silver of a mountain torrent, the
exquisite patterns of snow crystals, the creations of
artists.

Not by bread alone, but by the sweet song of a
mockingbird, the rustle of the wind in the trees, the
magic of a violin, the sublimity of a softly lighted
cathedral.

Not by bread alone, but by the fragrance of roses, the scent of orange blossoms, the smell of new-mown hay, the clasp of a friend's hand, the tenderness of a mother's kiss.

Not by bread alone, but by the lyrics of poets, the wisdom of sages, the holiness of saints, the biographies of great souls.

Not by bread alone, but by comradeship and high adventure, seeking and finding, serving and sharing, loving and being loved.

Man does not live by bread alone, but by being faithful in prayer, responding to the guidance of the Holy Spirit, finding and doing the loving will of God now and eternally.[6]

—*The University Presbyterian*

In the culinary world today we get the impression that all there is to live for is the next meal, the next night out, the next gourmet restaurant; we think that all there is to live for is bread. However, the Scriptures tell us very plainly that we do not live by bread alone. What are we to live for? Everything that proceeds out of the mouth of the Lord: beauty, harmony, truth, goodness, recreation, affection, friendships, aspirations, and worship. We become observers of the goodness of God and all His creation.

Prayer   *Father God, open my eyes to see beyond the physical needs of the day. Let me see vividly that I don't just live for bread. You have made such a vast universe I want to explore. Expand my mind to encompass all Your creations. Amen.*

Action   Write down several things that you observe of God's creation that you normally may not see or pay attention to (the colors of sunset, the beauty of the ocean or beach, the mountains, a stream, the sound of a bird). Close your eyes and appreciate God's handiwork.

Reflections

Lord of all pots and pans and things,
Since I've no time to be
A saint by doing lovely things
Or watching late with Thee,
Or dreaming in the dawnlight
Or storming heaven's gates,
Make me a saint by getting meals
And washing up the plates.

Thou who didst love to give men food
In room or by the sea,
Accept this service that I do—
I do it unto Thee.

—AUTHOR UNKNOWN

Perhaps the greatest social service that can be rendered by anybody to this country and to mankind is to bring up a family.

—George Bernard Shaw

Listen

*Let everyone be quick to hear, slow to
speak and slow to anger.*

—JAMES 1:19

*G*od in His great wisdom created mankind with two ears and only one mouth. I'm sure that was because He wanted us to listen twice as much as we speak. Most of us are very poor listeners. Bob and I rate this skill as one of the top priorities in having a good relationship. I guarantee that if couples would take the time to become better listeners their relationships would be improved through better understanding and increased patience. (It's important to remember, though, that women tend to be better listeners than men, probably because most men immediately want to fix what is broken and listening is considered a waste of time. To them, the solution is what's important; they want to go directly to the bottom line.)

So be brave and ask several of your trusted friends how they would rate you on your listening skills. Be prepared to take their honest answers and act upon the information constructively. Don't get into the trap of thinking you are much better at listening than so-and-so. Almost everyone is below par in this skill.

We will become better listeners when we realize how people value being heard. It gives people an awareness that we care for what they have to say and that we truly love them. Our own spirits are lifted up when those around us know we care for them.

Listening is truly an art form that can be mastered if we practice. Observe yourself in a crowd, or even one-on-one, to see how you do. Change comes when you know the truth.

Prayer

Father God, I know that I get into trouble with my relationships when I stop listening and start to open my mouth. Please forgive me for the words that I have said foolishly over the years. Heal the wounds I have left behind. I want to improve my relationships—let it begin today with me. Amen.

Action

Seek out a few friends and have them reflect on what kind of listener you are. Be brave and loving and willing to hear what they have to say.

Reflections

The Secret of the Wise Man

Behold, Thou dost desire truth in the innermost being,
and in the hidden part Thou wilt make
me know wisdom.

—PSALM 51:6

ecently I was driving down one of our busy freeways in Southern California when a sign suddenly appeared before me that read, "What the fool does at the end, wise men do at the beginning." I don't know how I was able to glimpse this since I was driving by, but my mind affirmed that this slogan has so much meaning.

We live in a day when humanity has sold out to secular materialism, a day when many people have put God on hold. The attitude of "I can do it myself; I don't need help from anyone—especially from a God I can't see or touch" rules. But as time goes by, many older people seem to get more wisdom after they have found that their paths have given them little meaning in life. As they ponder mortality, they often realize that the simplicity of their youth offered a peace and meaning that they rejected all through life. Wise people, on the other hand, have adopted the fear of

God at a young age. They have studied the wisdom of Scripture and applied it to their value structure.

Wisdom comes from knowing God and understanding His will for our lives. The Holy Spirit assists us in our quest for wisdom by enabling us to view the world as God perceives it. From an early age we can seek God's wisdom. We don't have to wait until we are old to figure out this puzzle of life. In Psalm 111:10 we read, "The fear of the LORD is the beginning of wisdom; a good understanding have all those who do His commandments; His praise endures forever."

Don't put off until tomorrow what you can do today. A wasted lifetime is a sham. Go to the cross of Jesus and trust Him with the simplicity of childlike faith.

Prayer   *Father God, I don't want to wait until I'm very old to exhibit Your traits of wisdom. I want a whole life of trusting You and Your word. May I also be able to transmit this desire to my family. Bless me as I put my faith into Your hands. Amen.*

Action   Ask God for the wisdom to walk in righteousness.

Reflections

Don't Quit

Do you not know that those who run in a race all run,
but only one receives the prize? Run in such a way
that you may win.

—1 Corinthians 9:24

Even though I don't consider myself athletic, I do enjoy a good sporting event. I like to see the heat of the game, the sweat of accomplishment, and the awareness of the necessary training to be a winner. I'm often prejudiced between sports that are individual in nature versus those that require teamwork. I prefer team sports because, as a mom, I sense that I'm a team player. I just love it when my whole family contributes to the success of our team, but I also feel like quitting when it seems like I'm carrying the whole load.

There have been times in my Christian walk when I've felt let down by others. I've been tempted to let up and quit, wondering if it is really worth it. However, David Hubbard has written some choice words just for me—and you:

> The program of God through history is like a relay race. Let one runner drop out and the whole team loses. Let one runner lose the baton and the whole team is eliminated. Let one runner break

the rules and the whole team is disqualified. The work of no runner counts until every runner does his share and the anchor man has hit the tape at the finish line.

The phrase "let us keep our eyes fixed on Jesus" is the key. The idea is clear. There are lots of distractions we run by: bypaths beckon us, false goals attract us, competition discourages us, and opposition causes us to falter. Jesus, however, a tried and trusted leader who blazed the trail of faith by His own obedience and perseverance and who finished the course in a burst of glory is both our guide and our goal. We look away from everything else but Him if we want to run well.[7]

Prayer   *Father God, may I always keep my eyes upon You. May I not become distracted along the way. I want to finish the race as a victor, and I know the only way to accomplish that is not to give up. Amen.*

Action   When have you felt like quitting? What did you do to get back on track?

Reflections

Happiness Is

If anyone wishes to come after Me, let him deny himself,
and take up his cross, and follow Me. For whoever wishes to
save his life shall lose it; but whoever loses his life for
My sake shall find it.

—MATTHEW 16:24,25

As I've been pondering the subject of happiness this morning—an elusive and seemingly unattainable state for so many—I am led to these words of Jesus from today's verse.

I believe the secret of happiness lies embedded in those words, painful though they appear to be. How else can we explain radiant people like the young man who sat in our living room and described how his six-year-old boy had died in his arms from leukemia. Today this man finds fulfillment in giving himself totally to helping college students. Or the woman I visited recently whose husband had turned out to be a homosexual and demanded a divorce. Some years later, this woman also lost her eyesight. Yet she is a cheerful, loving person, fully self-supporting.

You might say that such people almost have a right to be unhappy. That they are not lies in the way they spend themselves for others.

I have observed that when any of us embarks on the pursuit of happiness of ourselves, it eludes us. Often I've asked myself why. It must be because happiness comes to us only as a dividend. When we become absorbed in something demanding and worthwhile above and beyond ourselves, happiness seems to be there as a by-product of the self-giving.[8]

Catherine Marshall so captures the secrets of happiness found in serving others. When women tell me they are unhappy and that they have no purpose in life, I automatically know they have not humbled themselves to giving to others. People who are looking for people to serve them are usually unhappy. Happiness eludes us if we are looking for it in all the wrong places.

I encourage you to discover one of the secrets to contentment. Wake up each day to see whom you can serve. (Remember, it's important to serve with no expectations to be served back.)

Prayer   *Father God, may I be so engrossed in serving You that my dividend is happiness. I don't want to search for it because I may not find it. I know You are the giver of happiness—so I will serve You. Amen.*

Action   What are you doing today that gives you happiness?

Reflections

□ □ □

Make a Date
with Yourself

There is an appointed time for everything.
And there is a time for every event under heaven.

—ECCLESIASTES 3:1

What would we do without our day planners? I have a large one for my desk and a carry-all that goes with me. I don't know how a person functions without some type of organizer. I just love it; it truly has become my daily-calendar bible. I take it with me everywhere. My whole life is in that book. Each evening I peek in to see what tomorrow has to bring. I just love to see a busy calendar; it makes me feel so alive. I've got this to do and that to do.

Then I come upon a day that has all white space. Not one thing to do. *What, oh what will I do to fill the space and time?* That's the way I used to think and plan. All my spaces had appointments written down and many times they even overlapped.

I now plan for white spaces. I even plan ahead weeks or months and black out "saved for me or my family" days. I have begun to realize that there are precious times for myself and my loved ones. Bob and I really try to protect these saved spaces just for us. We may not go anywhere or do anything out of the ordinary, but it's our special time. We can do anything we want: sleep in, stay out late, go to lunch, read a book, go to a movie, or take a nap. I really look forward with great anticipation when these white spaces appear on my calendar.

I've been so impressed when I've read biographies of famous people. Many of them are controllers of their own time. They don't let outsiders dictate their schedules. Sure, there are times when things have to be done on special days, but generally that isn't the case. When we begin to control our calendars, we will find that our lives are more enjoyable and that the tensions of life are more manageable. Make those white spaces your friend, not your enemy.

Prayer   *Father God, let me be at peace when I see those white spaces on my calendar. May I be so bold as to create my own white spaces. I know that my body needs to be recharged and those free times are great for my spiritual, mental, and physical well being. Amen.*

Action   Flip to your calendar and create three white spaces just for you.

Reflections

No One Understands Like Jesus

And as for you, you meant evil against me,
but God meant it for good in order to bring about
this present result, to preserve many people alive.

—GENESIS 50:20

Since World War II, the name John W. Peterson has become synonymous with fine gospel music. Over 1,000 gospel songs and hymns, as well as many other musical works such as cantatas, anthems, choral arrangements, and gospel film musicals, have been written by this gifted and dedicated composer. Mr. and Mrs. Peterson gave this account of "No One Understands Like Jesus," written during the early years of John's ministry.

At one time I had a fairly responsible position with a well-known gospel ministry. One day a supervisory position opened up in my department. I was led to believe that I was to be promoted to this position. I was thrilled and challenged by the prospect of a new job. But I was bypassed, and a man from the outside was brought in to fill the position. There followed days of agonizing heart searching. It was all I could do to keep from becoming bitter. One night I had occasion to spend an evening with the man who was brought in for "my" position. For some reason or other, though otherwise a very pleasant fellow, that night he became quite caustic in some of his remarks to me, and I was deeply hurt. Later that evening, after returning home, I was sitting in our living room thinking about the events of the past days and about the bitter experiences of that evening. I began to feel very alone and forsaken. Suddenly, I sensed the presence of the Lord in an unusual way, and my mind was diverted from my difficulties to His faithfulness and sufficiency. Soon the thought occurred to me that He fully understood and sympathized with my situation—in fact, no one could ever completely understand or care as did He. Before long, the idea for the song came and I began to write.

No one understands like Jesus. He's a friend beyond compare; meet Him at the throne of mercy; He is waiting for you there.

No one understands like Jesus; ev'ry woe He sees and feels; tenderly He whispers comfort, and the broken heart He heals.

No one understands like Jesus when the foes of life assail; you should never be discouraged; Jesus cares and will not fail.

No one understands like Jesus when you falter on the way; tho you fail Him, sadly fail Him, He will pardon you today.

Refrain: No one understands like Jesus when the days are dark and grim; no one is so near, so dear as Jesus—cast your ev'ry care on Him.[9]

Prayer

Father God, You truly are the one who understands when I feel hurt and defeated. Where others have been cruel or unkind, You intended it for good to bring about this present result. Help me take today's trials and disappointments and make victories out of them. Amen.

Action

If you know the tune, sing all four stanzas of John Peterson's great song "No One Understands Like Jesus."

Reflections

Do all the good you can
By all the means you can,
In all the ways you can,
In all the places you can,
At all the times you can,
To all the people you can,
As long as ever you can.

—JOHN WESLEY

I Am with You in Spirit

For I, on my part, though absent in body
but present in spirit, have already
judged him who has so committed this,
as though I were present.

—1 CORINTHIANS 5:3

*U*sing this passage, today we will explore the idea of friendship and having the same spirit. There are friends who are closer than a brother or sister. Susan L. Lengkes writes:

> One of the most heart-rending moments of life comes when close friends say goodbye, knowing that many miles will separate them from their countless shared experiences. Distance takes on the menacing look of an enemy when it dares to stand between such friends!
>
> Soon they will find themselves building protective shields around the ache of separation. They will feel themselves both courting and resisting the urge to clip those threads that bind their hearts in love. And they will argue repeatedly with a voice that warns, "Don't build new friendships—life has a demolition crew around every corner!"
>
> But discovery lies ahead. Real friendship is resilient. The very cords that make it strong—commitment,

creativity, caring and sharing—are elastic, and friends can remain committed and even more creative in their long-distance sharing.

Now cards and letters—stackable memories to be relived over a cup of coffee—will communicate love in indelible ink. Now calls—where the value of every word, enhanced by the coming bill—will set precious priorities and release sentiment from the soul. Anticipated visits will be far richer for their infrequency. Thoughts and feelings long saved and protected will be unlocked and shared.

Best of all, a discovery will be made that hearts in harmony can just as easily carry a tune long-distance.[10]

During my present illness I have witnessed in real life what it means to be with friends in spirit. Not a day goes by that I don't receive cards from people like you that express their love and concern for me. I can't always remember names or faces, but my heart is melted by the fact that people are praying for me. At times I feel so undeserving of kind thoughts, but I'm reminded that having kindred spirits has everlasting benefits. I have a huge wicker basket in my office that I use to collect all the reminders that women out there are loving me through prayer and by sending cards. Tears come to my eyes daily for what God is doing to me through the confirmation of friends who care. Even though I have had to say goodbye to many people, they are really only a short distance away.

Prayer   *Father God, I fall at Your feet in amazement that women will pause in their busy schedules to pray for my physical, emotional, and spiritual well-being. There is no stronger force than those that have Christ-centered kindred spirits. Amen.*

Action   Call or write a friend who has moved away from you. Let your friend know you are praying for him or her.

Reflections

Look out for the interests of others.
You can't solve all the
world's problems, but you
can—and are called upon to—
help those whom God has placed
in your life.

—AUTHOR UNKNOWN

---

*Real joy comes not from ease or riches
or from the praise of men, but from
doing something worthwhile.*

—WILFRED T. GRENFELL

Life Is More Than Abundance

*Beware, and be on your guard against every
form of greed; for not even when one has an abundance
does his life consist of his possessions.*

—LUKE 12:15

One of our universal problems is the over-crowding of our homes. Whether we have an apartment or a six-bedroom home every closet, cupboard, refrigerator, and garage are all crammed with abundance. Some of us have so much that we go out and rent additional storage sheds for our possessions.

Bob and I are no different than you. We buy new clothes and cram them into our wardrobes. A new antique goes in the corner, a new quilt hangs over the bed, a new potted plant gathers sunlight by the window. On and on it goes. Pretty soon we feel as though we are closed in with no room to breathe. We continually struggle to keep a balance in our attitudes regarding possessions.

It is very simple to manage if you are single and live alone—it's just you. Life becomes more complicated with a spouse and children. You soon get that "bunched in" feeling. This creates more stress and you can lose your cool and blow relationships when your calm is broken.

We made a rule in our home about abundance. Simply stated it says, "One comes in and one goes out." After every purchase we gave away or sold a like item. (We have an annual garage sale.) With a new blouse out goes an older blouse, with a new table out goes a table, and so on. Naturally if you're a newlywed this rule is not for you because you probably don't have an abundance of possessions.

There's another strategy that's very effective. We have informed our loved ones that we don't want anymore gifts that take up space or that have to be dusted; we prefer receiving consumable items. Remember—your life is not based on your possessions. Share with others what you aren't using.

Prayer   *Father God, help me incorporate this new principle in my life. I don't want to be stressed out in this life because I own too much. Let me learn to be a giver and not a taker of possessions. I need help in this area of my life. Amen.*

Action   The next time you purchase an item of abundance, give a like item away or store it in your "future garage sale bag."

Reflections

One Who Walks
in Integrity

*A righteous [woman] who walks in [her] integrity—how
blessed are [her] sons after [her].*

—PROVERBS 20:7

My Bob often says, "Just do what you say you are going to do!" This has been our battle cry for more than 35 years. People get into relational problems because they forget to keep their promises. It's so easy to make a verbal promise for the moment, and then grapple with the execution of that promise later.

Sometimes we underestimate the consequences of not keeping the promise flippantly made in a moment of haste. Many times we aren't even aware that we have made a promise. Someone says, "I'll call you at 7:00 tonight, or I'll drop by before noon, or I'll call you to set up a breakfast meeting on Wednesday." Then the weak excuses begin to follow. "I called but no one answered" (even though you have voice mail and no message was left). "I got tied up and forgot." "I was too tired."

I suggest that we don't make promises if we aren't going to keep them. The person on the other end would prefer not hearing a promise that isn't going to be kept.

Yes, there will be times when the execution of a promise will have to be rescheduled, but be up-front with the person when you call to change the time frame. We aren't perfect, but we can mentor proper relationship skills to our friends and family by exhibiting accountability with our words of promise. We teach people that we are trustworthy—and how they can be trusted too.

You'll be surprised how people will pleasantly be surprised when you keep your promises. As my friend Florence Littauer says, "It takes so little to be above average." When you develop a reputation for being a woman who does what she says, your life will have more meaning and people will enjoy being around you.

Prayer   *Father God, I want to be a person others can trust when I make a promise. Let me examine my words to make sure I only give promises to others when I'm committed to fulfill what I've uttered. Truly, keeping promises reflects on my Christian witness. Convict me to be true to my words. Amen.*

Action   Carry out today the promises you made yesterday.

Reflections

That Inner Feeling

The LORD has done what He purposed; He has accomplished His word.

—LAMENTATIONS 2:17

I often have an instinctive feeling that something isn't right, that I should do this or that, but I usually pass on this because peer pressure tells me my inner feelings should be ignored. The older I become, the more I realize that living from my heart has value.

I don't want to get into the trap of following everyone else because it's the group thing to do. I want to live a life that is meaningful to me and my family. I want my decisions to be based on my Christian values. I want to use these values to help me make major decisions, not what TV, Madison Avenue, or popular newsstand magazines tell me to do or think.

In order to live intuitively one must have some quiet times to read and think. Hectic lives don't permit one to hear the heartbeat of the soul. When we are too busy we don't have time to dwell on the important issues in life.

I find that when I'm rushed I have an inner disturbance that prevents me from making well-thought-out decisions. When you and I are hurried in life, we have a tendency to have a deep anger inside because we forget to have time for ourselves. Our personal growth comes to a standstill.

During my recent illness I have had more and more time to reflect upon the important issues of life. God has put a stop to my go-go-go lifestyle, and He has told me to read, think, and dwell upon what my heart knows to be true. I'm more in tune with the beat of my heart and soul.

Prayer

Father God, let me be more aware of the feelings of my heart. You have given me so many of the desires of my heart, and I want to be more sensitive to what You are teaching me about life. I search for a solitude of peace and tranquility so I can hear Your thoughts in my heart. Amen.

Action

Ask yourself, "How do I really want to live my life?" Begin to act on your answer to this question.

Reflections

□ □ □

Castles in the Sand

For no man can lay a foundation other than the
one which is laid, which is Jesus Christ.

—1 CORINTHIANS 3:11

Each Fourth of July the city of Newport Beach, California, sponsors a huge sand-castle building contest. Our family has had the opportunity to observe this spectacle for several years. Men, women, and children arrive early with shovels, buckets, and trowels in hand to spend the whole day sculpturing magnificent structures out of sand. It's absolutely amazing to watch the teamwork that goes on. Each person seems to know what to do next. One of the hardest jobs is to go to the water's edge and bring back buckets of water to put on the sand structure. (Wet sand is a must.) The creative team members are the sculpturers who take a pile of sand and begin to form their sand-castle vision. Medieval castles with turrets, drawbridges, and protective moats are very popular. As the judges take their positions, the crowd waits with anticipation. Who will be the winners?

The last few hours of the day are spent watching the beautiful creations. That is, until the tide begins to advance and the waves begin to nibble at these gorgeous structures until they are all flattened and washed back into the ocean.

This is a great reminder for us to make sure that our efforts here on earth are everlasting—made with the gold, silver, and precious stones of our hearts and not with the perishable materials of wood, hay, and straw.

Prayer   *Father God, I want my life to mean more than building castles in the sand. I know they look beautiful, but I also realize they aren't eternal in nature. Help me to evaluate what is everlasting so that I will live on in the eyes of my children and grandchildren because of what was of value to me. Amen.*

Action   Take time today to evaluate your life and see if it's going to survive the forces of the waves in your life. What kind of building materials are you using to build your home? Are there a few areas that need remodeling?

Reflections

If you built castles in the air your work need not be lost; that is where they should be. Now put foundations under them.

—Henry David Thoreau

Three Sweet Words

Beloved, let us love one another, for love is from God;
and everyone who loves is born of
God and knows God.

—1 JOHN 4:7

ave you ever hungered after love? When my father, who was an alcoholic, was alive I would hope that he would come home with love in his heart rather than the anger he often exhibited. As a young girl I would have so cherished those three big words, "I love you." I guess that's one of the first reasons I was so attracted to my Bob. He came from a warm family that was very free in their expressions of endearment.

Over the years I, too, have made it a habit to say, "I love you." Saying these difficult words (I say difficult because the world finds them so hard to utter) has been very beneficial to me: It helps me feel good inside; it makes me realize that I'm a giver and not just a taker.

When our loved ones hear these words they certainly erase all the mistakes we've made recently. I often catch myself saying "I love you" as I hang up from talking to a friend or family member. You know what? After a while they return the forgotten words "I love you." There are many opportunities during the day to express that precious sentence.

Individuals who know they are loved have a cheerier outlook on life. There is a sparkle in their eyes, and they can look you eye-to-eye with a face that reflects confidence. This inner peace will radiate in all of their relationships. It is most difficult to not like someone who says that they love you. In fact it is almost impossible to do so.

The Scriptures are quite clear that God is love, and when we don't love we can't know God intimately. How often have we known a person for just a short time and know that we are kindred spirits? Why? Because he or she radiates the love of God. God's light truly shines.

Prayer   *Father God, may I be known by those around me as being a person who knows how to say "I love you." May my family never be able to accuse me of not telling them that I love them. I want to freely give these words to those I know. Amen.*

Action   Today tell five people that you love them.

Reflections

Examine Your Heart

And I shall give them one heart, and shall put a new spirit within them. And I shall take the heart of stone out of their flesh and give them a heart of flesh.

—Ezekiel 11:19

An engine with all its cylinders working properly can propel large trucks to their destinations; a neglected engine may not be able to move a vehicle out of the parking lot. So it is with the people of God. Worship is the engine that drives our relationship with God and with other believers. As we worship God with an undivided heart, we are better able to accomplish God's will in all facets of our lives. Let us take time to examine our heart and give to God the pure worship that He deserves.

Marcia Hare (1798–1870) prayed that she would be released from the bondage of an idol worshiping heart:

O Lord God Almighty, redeem my soul from its bondage, that I may be free to live hence forth, not for myself; but for you. Help me to put away self, and to remember that this life is not given for my ease, my enjoyment. It is a schooling time for the eternal home you have prepared for those who love you. Keep my eye steadily fixed on that haven of rest and peace, that I may not be faint nor be weary from the length of the way, but may strive to walk worthy of my high calling in all meekness and lowliness of heart. Amen.

I readily take note that what we do on this earth prepares us for eternity. In order for us to think in these terms requires us to have a heart of flesh (tenderness) and not of stone. In Ezekiel 11:20, the writer repeats what God told him about why we are to have a new heart: "that they may walk in My statutes and keep My ordinances, and do them. Then they will be My people, and I shall be their God." If people find it difficult to follow God's ordinances maybe it's because they still have hearts of stone; they need heart operations that will turn their stones to flesh.

Prayer   *Father God, I humbly bow down before You in worship. Tear down all the idols of my life and give me a tender heart that's 100 percent devoted to You. Teach me to obey Your commands as Your child. Amen.*

Action   Check your heart to see if it's made of stone or flesh. Which is it? What can you do to grow in your devotion to God?

Reflections

My Child's a Teenager!

*Train up a child in the way he should go, even when
he is old he will not depart from it.*

—PROVERBS 22:6

often hear from mothers that they are
dreading their children as teenagers as
if it's some kind of disease. This phase
of parental life has certainly received a bad rap over the
years. Parents have built in a great fear for this segment
of raising children. It's like all of a sudden we don't know
how to behave around them. They have unique physical features, they listen to funny music, their hairstyles
come out of a black hole, and their choices of friends can
certainly be questioned. What ever happened to the sweet,
young children who used to live in our homes? Most of us
have or will experience this particular transition phase of
our children.

After having had two teenagers of our own and now five
grandchildren who are standing at the "teen" door knocking, I want to encourage you with a few positive thoughts.
Remember that your children are God's children and that
He loves them unconditionally. Also remember that being
teenagers doesn't mean they will always be encased in this
block of time. It is a phase that will pass.

Don't be inclined to take everything they say or do
personally. They don't always mean what you hear. Be

positive toward them; hesitate to be negative because they will become who you think they are. If you accept them, they will be inclined to accept themselves.

Keep a great sense of humor; a smile or laugh will go a long way to set the tone around the home. Fortunately, children will not become the adults they are as teenagers.

Having teenagers will improve your prayer life—and that's not bad. Having a teenager will also make you a better parent and a better person.

Prayer   *Father God, You know I have real concerns about my child becoming a teenager. Encourage me to rise to the occasion and remain a loving and accepting mother. Remind me that this is a phase and not etched in stone. Thank You. Amen.*

Action   Hug a teenager today and let that person know how much you love him or her.

Reflections

To nourish children and raise them against odds is in any time, any place, more valuable than to fix bolts in cars or design nuclear weapons.

—MARILYN FRENCH

Allow the Master Potter to Mold You

*But the vessel that he was making of clay was spoiled in
the hand of the potter; so he remade it into another vessel,
as it pleased the potter to make.*

—JEREMIAH 18:4

Because I love to collect beautiful teacups
and saucers, I love a little parable someone shared with me years ago. I have
taken this little tale by an unknown author and retold it in
a way that speaks most deeply to me about my own pain
and my own transformation.

The story begins in a little gift shop, a charming estab-
lishment crammed full of delightful discoveries. A man
and a woman have gone there to find a special gift for
their granddaughter's birthday. With excited oohs and
ahs, they pick up dolls and books and figurines, intent
on finding just the perfect piece. Suddenly, glancing into
the corner of an antique armoire, the grandmother spies
a prize.

"Oh, honey, look!" she exclaims, taking him by
the arm and pointing. Carefully he reaches over to
pick up a delicate teacup in his big hand. A shaft of

sunlight from the window shines through the trans-
lucent china, illuminating the delicate design.

"Oh, isn't it pretty?" the grandmother sighs.

He nodded. "I don't know much about dishes,
but I'd have to say that's the best-looking cup I've
ever seen."

Together they gaze at the beautiful little cup,
already imagining their granddaughter's face when
she opens her special gift. And at that moment
something remarkable happens: With a voice as
clear and sweet as the painted nosegay on the
saucer, that teacup begins to talk.

"I thank you for the compliment," the cup
begins, "but you know, I haven't always been like
this."

A little shaken at being addressed by a teacup,
the grandfather places it back on the shelf and takes
a step back. But his wife doesn't seem surprised at
all. Instead, she asks with interest, "Whatever are
you talking about?"

"Well," says the teacup, "I wasn't always beautiful. In fact, I started out as an ugly, soggy lump
of clay. But one day a man with dirty, wet hands
started slinging me around, pounding me on the
worktable, knocking the breath out of me. I didn't
like this procedure one little bit. It hurt, and it made
me angry.

"Stop!" I cried.

"But the man with the wet hands simply said,
'Not yet!' "

"Finally the pounding stopped, and I breathed
a sigh of relief. I thought my ordeal was over. But it
had just begun.

"The next thing I knew, I was being stuffed into a
mold—packed in so tightly I couldn't see straight.

"'Stop! Stop!'" I cried until I was squeezed too tight to utter a sound. Parts of me oozed out of the mold, and he scraped those away.

"If I could have talked, I would have screamed.

"But the man seemed to know what I was thinking. He just looked down with a patient expression on his face and told me, "'Not yet.'"

"Finally, the pressing and the scraping stopped. But the next experience was far worse. I was plunged into the dark, and then the temperature began to rise. The air grew hotter and hotter, until I was in agony. I still couldn't talk, but inside I was yelling, 'Get me out of here!'

"And strangely, through those thick furnace walls, I seemed to hear someone say, 'Not yet.'

"Just when I was sure I was going to be completely incinerated, the oven began to cool. Eventually the man took me out of the furnace and released me from that confining mold. I relaxed. I even looked around and enjoyed my new form. I was firmer. I had shape. This was better.

"But then came the short lady in the smock. She pulled out tiny brushes and began to daub paint all over me. The fumes made me feel sick, and the brush tickled.

"'I don't like that,'" I cried. "'I've had enough. Please stop.'"

"'Not yet!'" said the short lady with a smile.

"Finally she finished. She picked up her brushes and moved on. But just when I thought I was finally free, the first man picked me up again and put me back into that awful furnace. This time was worse than before because I wasn't protected by the mold.

"Again and again I screamed, 'Stop!'

"And each time the man answered through the door of the furnace, 'Not yet!'

"Finally the oven cooled once more, and the man came to open the door. By that time I was almost done in. I barely noticed when I was picked up and put down and packed in a box and jounced and jolted some more. When I finally came to, a pretty lady was picking me up out of my box and placing me on this shelf, next to this mirror.

"And when I looked at myself in the mirror, I was amazed. No longer was I ugly, soggy, and dirty. I was shiny and clean. And I was beautiful—unbelievably beautiful. 'Could this be me?' I cried for joy.

"It was then," said the teacup, "that I realized there was a purpose in all that pain. You see, it took all that suffering to make me truly beautiful."[11]

God doesn't want to throw anyone into the corner. He didn't create us for that. He didn't empty Himself and come to earth in Christ Jesus for that. Our Lord didn't go to the cross for that; He didn't rise from the dead for that. God doesn't want broken pots. Our hope is that we remain open to the working of God in our lives, responding to God, allowing the Master Potter to do the beautiful work that He desires to do in each of us.

Prayer   Father God, keep me pliable and not hardened. This way You can mold me in Your way. Do Your perfect work in me. Amen.

Action   Find a beautiful teacup and put it somewhere so you'll see it everyday. On it place the words, "Because of You, Lord."

Reflections

Don't count how many years you've spent,
Just count the good you've done;
The times you've lent a helping hand,
The friends that you have won.
Count your deeds of kindness,
The smiles not the tears;
Count all the pleasures
That you've had
But never count the years.

—AUTHOR UNKNOWN

---

*O Divine Master, grant that I may
not so much seek to be consoled as to console;
to be understood as to understand;
to be loved as to love; for it is in giving
that we receive; it is in pardoning
that we are pardoned;
and it is in dying that we
are born to Eternal Life.*

—FRANCIS OF ASSISI

I Will Give Thanks

I will give thanks to Thee, O Lord my God,
with all my heart, and will glorify
Thy name forever.

—PSALM 86:12

*P*raise God from whom all blessings flow; praise Him, all creatures here below; praise Him above, ye heavenly host; praise Father, Son, and Holy Ghost. Amen.

The lines of the "Doxology" have been the most frequently sung words of any known song for more than 300 years. Even today most English-speaking Protestant congregations unite at least once each Sunday in this noble overture of praise. It has been said that the Doxology has done more to teach the doctrine of the Trinity than all the theology books ever written.

Instead of being merely a hymn that is sung periodically, the "Doxology" should be regarded by Christians as an offering or sacrifice of praise to God for all His blessings in the past week (Hebrew 13:15).

The author of this text was a bold, outspoken seventeenth-century Anglican bishop named Thomas Ken.

Ken's illustrious career in the ministry was stormy and colorful. He served for a time as the English chaplain at the royal court in The Hague, Holland. He was so outspoken, however, in denouncing the corrupt lives of those in authority at the Dutch capital that he was compelled to leave after a short stay.

Upon his return to England, he was appointed by King Charles II to be one of his chaplains. Ken continued to reveal the same spirit of boldness in rebuking the moral sins of his dissolute English monarch. Despite this, Charles always admired his courageous chaplain, calling him "the good little man." The king rewarded Thomas Ken by appointing him to the bishopric of the Bath and Wales area. The historian Macaulay gave this tribute to Bishop Ken: "He came as near to the ideal of Christian perfection as human weakness permits."[12]

Prayer   Father God, I sing this Doxology as a prayer of commitment to You. I want to always praise You—the Father, Son, and Holy Ghost. Amen.

Action   Sing the Doxology with all the gusto you can (as if you were in the shower).

Reflections

☐ ☐ ☐

Live Each Day to Its Fullest

*Always giving thanks for all things in the
name of our Lord Jesus Christ to God,
even to the Father.*

—EPHESIANS 5:20

ecause of my recent illness, I've spent a lot of time waiting in the reception areas of doctors' offices. (In most cases the wait was at least an hour after my scheduled appointment.) During this time I have the opportunity to talk to people who have been diagnosed with a disease that will shorten their life expectancies—in short they have received "bad news." In this course of events I have become aware that I no longer want to wait for bad news before I begin to appreciate life. I've always been a thankful person with gratitude to God for what He has given me, but I'm now more dedicated to not taking for granted one single day of my existence because life can be very short. I don't want to postpone one day of thankfulness for the life I have; it is so precious.

Our situation can change at the drop of a hat. Bad news can come in a moment's notice. We have no promise that we will live forever; in fact, "it is appointed for men to die" (Hebrews 9:27). As I look around today, I can truly thank God abundantly for the simple things of life: sleep, walking, running, heartbeats, husband, children, grandchildren, peace, and so on. Things that I used to take for granted. But now I never want to give into the fear of what might come next, a fear of the unknown. I want to be grateful to God for all that He gives to me and my family. I find myself taking moments several times a day to thank God for all my blessings. I don't want to leave out the most minute reason for appreciation.

I think this time of uncertainty has been a wonderful experience for me because it has made me appreciate what I have. I'm far more aware of how bountiful my life is and has been. I truly have a thankful heart because of this season in my life. The glass is truly half-full and not half-empty.

Prayer   *Father God, I don't want to wait to receive bad news before I thank You. Make me aware of all my blessings before sickness or tragedy strikes. You are the giver of all goodness, and I thank You for all Your provisions. Amen.*

Action   Make it a daily habit to pause and give thanks to God for your many blessings.

Reflections

□ □ □

A Life of Blessings

*Blessed are the peacemakers, for they shall
be called sons of God.*

—MATTHEW 5:9

History is full of people who have been peacemakers. They have been willing to risk their well-being, health, and wealth to stand in the gap between separated parties to help heal disagreements and avoid wars. Even within families we can witness the terrible destruction that takes place between warring members. Sometimes the road seems to be strewn with fragmented lives. But Jesus is quite clear that He wants *all* of His children to be known as peacemakers. Scripture makes it plain that we are to be known as ambassadors of peace toward:

- *God:* "God has given us the task of reconciling people to him" (2 Corinthians 5:18 NLT).
- *Ourselves:* "Joy fills hearts that are planning peace!" (Proverbs 12:20 NLT).
- *Others:* "And those who are peacemakers will plant seeds of peace and reap a harvest of goodness" (James 3:18 NLT).

Since the blessing of being a peacemaker is to be called a child of God, we can experience the joy of goodness, happiness, and peace within our own lives. When we exhibit these positive traits we will begin to reflect:

- *Contentment with ourselves:* We will know who we are in Christ, thus giving us the contentment we have long searched for.

- *Optimism in our faith:* We will exhibit a love for God and reflect a positive faith in how we look at life and the events that come our way.

- *Relationally connectedness:* We will have deeper friendships. People will be bonded closer to us. We will become better friends.

- *Mercy:* We will be more willing and capable of giving mercy in our dealings with ourselves and others.

- *Doing what is right:* We will have a benchmark to judge proper behavior for ourselves.

Make Jesus your Savior and become a peacemaker.

Prayer   *Father God, may I have the courage to step out and become a peacemaker. Let it start with me and ripple out to others that I meet. Help me humble myself so that I can be lifted up and used for Your kingdom. Amen.*

Action   Bury the hatchet that causes war within yourself and with others. Take your sins to the cross and leave them there, never to pick them up again.

Reflections

□ □ □

Interview Your Friends

*A man of many friends comes to ruin, but there is a
friend who sticks closer than a brother.*

—PROVERBS 18:24

A good paraphrase of our opening Scripture is: A woman of too many friends will be broken in pieces. Indiscriminately chosen friends may bring trouble, but a genuine friend sticks with you through thick and thin.

Our friends have a positive or negative effect upon our lives. And many of us have told our children to be careful who they run with because people are known by the company they keep. There are certain areas in our lives that keep us from choosing who we are around, such as work, church, neighbors, and social clubs. In these settings we are thrown together. However, in our family and private times we can be very discriminate with whom we associate. We must realize that our time and energy are among our most precious assets. Therefore it's important to make wise choices in our selection of people we will spend time with. Are they people who build us up and encourage us to be better people than we would be by ourselves?

Why have you chosen the people who are closest to you? How do they contribute to who you are? It's not that you cast off those who don't contribute positively to your life, but you might evaluate their part in contributing to who you are. I encourage you to reevaluate and see how you respond when you are around certain people. Do you respect them? Do they encourage you to grow? Do you have a kindred spirit? Do you share like values? If you can't answer to the affirmative, you might want to review how much time you spend with these people. Some changes might be in order.

You have a limited amount of time to spend with others, so select wisely; much of who you are—positive as well as negative—will be formed by the friends you keep.

Prayer   Father God, thank You for the wonderful group of friends I have. You have brought into my life such a great support system. Even though I can't give each equal time, they are there supporting me in daily prayer. I appreciate how You have screened out negative influences and present me with those who will love and lift me up. Amen.

Action   Evaluate why certain people are your friends. Do you need to make any changes?

Reflections

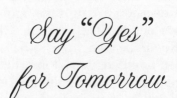

Say "Yes" for Tomorrow

Rejoice that your names are recorded in heaven.

—LUKE 10:20

A few days after Roy Rogers passed away at his home in Apple Valley, California a local Christian television station ran a tribute to his life. One of the segments had Dale Evans, Roy's wife, singing a song entitled, "Say 'Yes' for Tomorrow." This song was dedicated to the memory of Roy's early decision to put his trust in Jesus as his Savior. While listening to this song I began to think back over my own life, back to when I invited Jesus, as my Lord, into my heart. At that time I made the most important decision in my life. I truly said "Yes for tomorrow," in that I settled my eternity by saying "yes" to Jesus. I was a young 16-year-old teenager who came from a Jewish background. Even though my decision for Christ didn't set well with my extended family of aunts and uncles, it did settle for me what my tomorrows would be. My direction for the future was decided. As I've matured in my life I've realized that many adults have never made that affirmation. What a shame to search all one's life and then, at the end of life, be unsure what the future might hold.

Dale Evans was sharing with her audience that Roy had made this decision a long time ago. And since she is also a believer she has the assurance that she will be reunited with Roy in heaven.

If you haven't settled what tomorrow will be, take time today to guarantee your destination. Confirm to your family that you will be united together forever in heaven.

Prayer   *Father God, I thank You for providing a way so that I can know where my tomorrow will be. Thank You for sending Jesus to pay the price on the cross for my sins. I'm so glad I said "yes" as a young girl! Amen.*

Action   If you haven't answered the tomorrow question, today might be the day to settle the most important question in your life.

Reflections

A Child of the King

*The Spirit Himself bears witness with our spirit that
we are children of God.*

—ROMANS 8:16

Whether you are great or small in God's kingdom, you are still God's child. An infant is as truly a child of its parents as is a full-grown person. You are as dear to your heavenly Father as the most prominent member of His family.

Harriett Buell wrote the words for "A Child of the King" one Sunday morning while walking home from her Methodist church service. She sent her text to the *Northern Christian Advocate* magazine, and it was printed in the February 1, 1877 issue. John Sumner, a singer and school music teacher, saw the words and composed the music. The hymn has been widely used since then to remind believers who they really are—bearers of God's image (see Genesis 1:26) and children of the King of kings.

As children of the heavenly kingdom, we can enjoy and possess the rich spiritual blessings that belong to us as heirs of God's riches.

- We have been justified and made acceptable to God (Romans 5:1).

- We have been adopted into God's royal family

(Romans 8:16,17).

- We have been given a citizenship in heaven (Philippians 3:20).

- We possess the indwelling Holy Spirit (1 Corinthians 6:19).

- We have been placed into the kingdom of the Son of God's love (Colossians 1:13).

- We have the promise that the best is yet to come—a heavenly home (John 14:2,3).

My Father is rich in houses and lands; He holdeth the wealth of the world in His hands! Of rubies and diamonds, of silver and gold, His coffers are full—He has riches untold.

My Father's own son, the Savior of men, once wandered o'er earth as the poorest of them; but now He is reigning forever on high, and will give me a home in heav'n by and by.

I once was an outcast stranger on earth, a sinner by choice and an alien by birth! But I've been adopted; my name's written down—an heir to a mansion, a robe, and a crown.

A tent or a cottage, why should I care? They're building a palace for me over there! Tho exiled from home, yet still I may sing: All glory to God, I'm a child of the King.

Chorus: I'm a child of the King! I'm a child of the King! With Jesus, my Savior, I'm a child of the King![13]

Prayer

Father God, just to think that I am Your child makes me tremble with amazement. Just to think that I have Your riches because I'm one of Your heirs seems such a miracle. May I be an exceptional steward of all Your resources. Amen.

Action What is your response to the truths found in the Scriptures quoted in today's reading?

Reflections

There are two ways of spreading light:
to be the candle or the mirror
that receives it.

—EDITH WHARTON

Confident Living

*Home is the one place in all this world
where hearts are sure of each other.
It is the place of confidence. It is the place
where we tear off that mask of guarded and
suspicious coldness which the world forces us to
wear in self-defense, and where we pour out
the unreserved communication of full and
confiding hearts. It is the spot where expressions
of tenderness gush out without any dread
of sensation of awkwardness and without
any dread of ridicule.*

FREDERICK W. ROBERTSON

It's Okay to Be Selfish

You shall love your neighbor as yourself.

—Leviticus 19:18

Yes, I give you permission to be selfish at times. One thing that I notice about so many people is that they are burned out because they spend so much time serving others that they have no time for themselves. As a young mom I was going from sun-up to late in the evening just doing the things that moms do. When evening came around I was exhausted. All I wanted to do was take a hot bath and slip into bed and catch as much sleep as possible before I was awakened in the night by one of the children. Yes, my Bob helped me but there were certain things mom had to do. After several years I remember saying to myself, "I've got to have some time just for me—I need help." One of the things I did was to get up a half hour before everyone else so I could spend time in the Scriptures over an early cup of tea. This one activity had an incredibly positive effect upon my outlook. I went on to making arrangements to get my hair and nails taken care of periodically. I was even known to purchase a new outfit (on sale of course) occasionally. As I matured I discovered that I became a better parent and wife when I had time for myself and my emotional tank filled up. I soon realized that I had plenty left over to share with my loved ones.

When you are able to spend some time just for you, you will be more relaxed and your family and home will function better. These "selfish" rituals don't have to be long in duration. Sometimes short experiences pay big dividends. I find these to be beneficial time-outs:

- taking a cozy, warm bath with bath salts and a flickering candle
- getting a massage
- having my hair and nails done
- meeting a friend for lunch
- listening to my favorite CD
- reading a good book
- writing a poem
- getting cozy on the couch
- watching a classic movie

Prayer   *Father God, I want time for myself in such a big way, but I always thought it wasn't Christian to be selfish. Thanks for reminding me that it's okay to take time for me; I know I will be more loving to those around me. Amen.*

Action   Create an activity that is yours exclusively, something you do just for you.

Reflections

Lift Yourself Up

For Thou didst form my inward parts;
Thou didst weave me in my mother's womb....
I am fearfully and wonderfully made.

—PSALM 139:13,14

f I could only have a straight nose, a tummy tuck, blond hair, larger (or smaller) breasts, or be more like so-and-so, I would be okay as a person. Never have I heard women satisfied with how God made them.

"God must have made a mistake when He made me." "I'm certainly the exception to His model creation." "There's so much wrong with me, I'm just paralyzed with who I am."

These negative thoughts poison our system. We can't be lifted up when we spend so much time tearing ourselves down. When we are in a negative mode, we can always find verification for what we're looking for. If we concentrate on the negative, we lose sight of all the positive aspects of our lives. We can always justify our damaging assumptions when we overlook the good God has for us.

These critical vibes create more negative vibes. Soon we are in a downward spiral. When you concentrate on your imperfections you have a tendency to look at what's wrong and not what's right. Putting yourself down can have some severe personal consequences.

Have you ever realized that God made you uniquely different from everyone else? (Even if you're a twin you are different.) Yes, it is important to work on improving your imperfections—but don't dwell on them so much that you forget who you are in the sight of God. The more positive you are toward yourself the more you will grow into the person God had in mind for you when you were created. Go easy on yourself. Remember, none of us will ever be perfect. The only way we will improve our self-image is by being positive and acknowledging that we are God's creation. Negativity tears down; positivity builds up.

Prayer   *Father God, You knew me while I was in my mother's womb. I hunger to be the woman You created me to be. Help me become all that You had in mind when You made me. Cut off all my negative thoughts and expressions. I want others around me to know me as a positive person. I want to reflect Your love. Amen.*

Action   Write down five negative thoughts about yourself that you often have. Beside each one list the positive aspects of those imperfections. Pray about them. From now on verbalize and think on just the positive.

Reflections

□ □ □

Be an Example

Proving to be examples to the flock...

—1 Peter 5:3

Over and over I have attempted to be an example by doing rather than telling. I feel that God's great truths are "caught" and not always "taught." In the book of Deuteronomy, Moses (the author) states, "You shall teach [God's commandment, the statutes, and the judgments] diligently to your sons and shall talk of them when you sit in your house and when you walk by the way and when you lie down and when you rise up" (6:7). In other words, at all times we are to be examples.

It is amazing how much we can teach by example in every situation: at home, at the beach, while jogging, when resting, when eating—in every part of the day. It's amazing how much I catch our children and grandchildren imitating the values that we exhibited in our home—something as little as a lighted candle to warm the heart to a "thank you" when food is being served in a restaurant.

Little eyes are peering out to see who our lives behave like when no one is looking. Are we consistent with what we say we believe? If we talk calmness and patience, how do we respond when standing in a slow line at the market? How does our conversation go when there is a

121

slowdown on Friday evening's freeway drive. Do we go by the rules on the freeway (having two people or more in the car while driving in the car-pool lane, going the speed limit, and obeying all traffic signs)?

How can we show God's love? By helping people out when they are in need of assistance, even when it is not convenient. We can be good neighbors. Sending out thank-you cards after receiving a gift shows our appreciation for the gift and the person. Being kind to animals and the environment when we go to the park for a camp-out or picnic shows good stewardship. We are continually setting some kind of example whether we know it or not.

Prayer   *Father God, let my life be an example to me as well as to those around me. May I exhibit proper conduct even when no one is around. I want to be obedient to Your guiding principles. Thank You for Your example. Amen.*

Action   Pick up some litter and throw it into a garbage can.

Reflections

□ □ □

Seeing Again

*They said to Him, "Lord we want our
eyes to be opened."*

—MATTHEW 20:33

wo blind men were sitting by the roadside in
Jericho. There is an oasis there—a good spring
and shade trees. Jesus was coming, and they
had hope. When He came near, they called, "Lord, have
mercy on us, Son of David!"

The story is short. Jesus healed them; He gave them
their sight. Their hope was fulfilled. "But I have my
spiritual eyesight," you say. Is there a story of hope for me
here? Look again. It isn't in the English translation, but it is
in the Greek: "They saw again." Again! They had not been
born blind; once they could see. They had seen beauty, the
sunlight, a child's smile, a loved one's look. But then it
all turned dark. Jesus came by and their hope came true:
They could see!

Have you known sight—real sight? You know what
it is to have been in God's sunlight enjoying His smile.
Have you given up hope of ever having that experience
again? No matter how long your sight has been fading
or how long you've sat by the side of life's spiritual road,
Jesus will touch you if you'll call on Him. You'll see
again. That's hope!14

Prayer   Father God, I truly want to see spiritually
                again. I thank You for the gift of having my
                eyes and good eyesight; however, I want to see
                things more clearly and vividly as I read your
                Scripture. Amen.

Action   Do you need a healing, spiritual touch?
                Ask God for that blessing.

Reflections

---

*I like not only to be loved, but to be told
that I am loved; the realm of silence is large
enough beyond the grave.*

—GEORGE ELIOT

It's Okay to Disagree

Make my joy complete by being of the same mind,
maintaining the same love, united in spirit,
intent on one purpose.

—PHILIPPIANS 2:2

For many years I thought a couple was never to disagree—that Bob and I, as a couple, should agree at all times. Then I began to realize that this wasn't always possible because Bob and I came from different backgrounds.

We can justify why we think a certain way because of the way we were raised. The problem with this line of thinking is that we both can justify our respective choices. We all tend to believe that the others in our lives should think like we do. But if this isn't true in real life, how can we always agree? Also, as I studied the basic temperament types, I soon realized that my Bob had a different temperament from me. This means we tend to respond differently to situations or ideas.

With this new data, Bob and I gave each other permission to disagree. We became better listeners and weren't so defensive and argumentative. With our new knowledge, we weren't as easily frustrated just because we didn't think alike. It was okay; we agreed to be able to disagree. What a freeing experience! With this agreement we seemed to respect each other's diversity in opinions more. I had a more loving attitude toward Bob because he looked at me in a different way—my ideas and concerns were more important.

Everyone wins in this outlook. Because of this arrangement, Bob and I are much more able to be united in one mind, one love, one spirit, and one purpose. To this day we are strongly committed to the real issues of life. In the big issues we are as one; in the lesser issues we still differ—and that's what makes marriage so much fun.

Prayer   *Father God, help me and my husband have the flexibility to agree to disagree. What a difference it will make in our marriage. Show me how I can have a greater tolerance for our differences and still be able to agree on the big issues of life. Thank You for making each of us unique and special. Amen.*

Action   Permit your spouse and friends to disagree with your value system. Be willing to listen to their thoughts and expressions.

Reflections

Be in Subjection

*Let every person be in subjection to the governing authorities.
For there is no authority except from God, and
those which exist are established by God.*

—ROMANS 13:1

There is no authority except from God. God establishes and upholds the principles of government even though some governments do not fulfill His desires.

We are at a very crucial time in American history when the Christian church can have a great impact on how this country will survive. We are to be cheerleaders for America; our children must be taught to be protectors of its heritage. Franklin D. Roosevelt once gave a speech entitled "The Four Freedoms." In it he stated:

> In the future days, which we seek to make secure, we look forward to a world founded upon four essential human freedoms:
>
> - The first is freedom of speech and expression.
> - The second is freedom of every person to worship God in his own way.
> - The third is freedom from want.
> - The fourth is freedom from fear.

Each of these basic freedoms is not only valued by Americans but by people all over the world. We no longer can think in national terms; we must think globally. Our world is shrinking in size, and who is our neighbor has been broadened in scope.

The greatness of America is founded not so much on what happens on a government level but on what happens in our homes. Our country needs great families; let it begin with you. Are we going to make a difference in the history of America?

Prayer   *"Father God, grant that not only the love of liberty but a thorough knowledge of the rights of man may pervade all nations of the earth, so that a philosopher may set his foot anywhere on its surface and say, 'This is my country.'"*

—A prayer given by
Benjamin Franklin

Action   At dinner tonight sing "America" after saying your blessing.

Reflections

The Wise Are Mature

*We are no longer to be children, tossed here and
there by waves, and carried about by every wind
of doctrine, by the trickery of men, by
craftiness in deceitful scheming; but
speaking the truth in love, we are to
grow up in all aspects into Him.*

—EPHESIANS 4:14,15

God does not want us to remain
spiritually immature. Many of the
30-to-50-year-old women I meet
seem to dwell on how old they are. There doesn't seem to
be much hope or time for them to make an impact in life.
I always reassure them how beautiful the older decades
are. Each season of life has so much to offer. Life becomes
richer the more mature we become.

Benjamine Jowett once wrote,

> Though I am growing old, I maintain that the
> best part is yet to come—the time when one may see
> things more dispassionately and know oneself and
> others more truly, and perhaps be able to do more,
> and in religion rest centered in a few simple truths.
> I do not want to ignore the other side that one will
> not be able to see so well or walk so far or read so
> much. But there may be more peace within, more

communications with God, more real light instead of distraction about many things, better relations with others, and fewer mistakes.

In our Christian walk we are encouraged not to remain as babes and children, but to wean ourselves off of spiritual milk and soft food and grow into healthier foods. God wants us to exhibit signs of maturity, and many times this comes through very difficult life situations. My experience validates that we grow through difficulties and not through just the good times.

If we are not mature, the reason is observable: We have not been workers but idlers in our study of the Bible. Those who are just "Sunday Christians" will never grow to maturity—it takes the study of the Scriptures to become meat-eaters of God's Word. We must be workers in the Scriptures. Paul told Timothy, "Be diligent to present yourself approved to God as a workman...handling accurately the word of truth" (2 Timothy 2:15). We must roll up our sleeves and do the job ourselves instead of expecting a pastor or teacher to do it for us.

Prayer   Father God, thank You for inspiring men of old to write Your Scriptures. They have become my Scriptures; they have become my salvation. Without the knowledge of Scripture my life would be tossed about like the waves in the wind. Thank You for my stability. Amen.

Action   Take a book of the Bible and begin reading a little each day. (If you're not sure where to start, I recommend the book of John in the New Testament.)

Reflections

□ □ □

Leave a Legacy

For I am mindful of the sincere faith within you,
which first dwelt in your grandmother Lois,
and your mother Eunice, and I am sure
that it is in you as well.

—2 TIMOTHY 1:5

Have you ever been challenged regarding what kind of legacy you are going to leave to your heirs? We all leave some type of belief system regardless of how we live our lives. It will either be good and positive or it will be bad and negative. Our heirs will reflect what kind of influence we had on their lives.

Paul writes this second letter to his friend Timothy and challenges him to remember the influence that his mother and grandmother had upon his life. In 2 Timothy 1:3-18 Paul encourages Timothy to concentrate on the past, present, and future aspects of developing a legacy. Paul wants Timothy to "fan the flame" of his faith for God. The character development Timothy needed was to embrace and live out the fact that God had not given him a spirit of timidity (cowardice) but one of power, love, and discipline.

The second part of the legacy was to follow the plan that God had given them. Paul warned Timothy that at times he might have to suffer for preaching the gospel.

131

He stressed not to be ashamed, but to believe and be convinced that Jesus is able to guard what has been entrusted to Him.

Another aspect of passing this legacy to others is to pattern our lives from what we have seen. Paul stressed that we retain the standard of sound words that we have heard from him. We are to guard, through the Holy Spirit, the treasure (gospel) that has been entrusted to us.

The last aspect of developing a worthwhile legacy is to pass it on. Paul told Timothy to entrust these truths to "faithful men who will be able to teach others also" (2 Timothy 2:1,2). Be a mom who cares about the kind of legacy you leave when the Lord calls you home. Teach your children these truths:

- Fan the flame of passion for God
- Follow God's plan for you
- Pattern your life from what you have learned
- Pass it on to those who will follow

Prayer *Father God, I want to pass on a godly legacy— one that will uphold the tenets of the gospel of the first century. Let me begin today to take life—and You—more seriously than I have. Amen.*

Action Develop a plan to pass on your faith to your loved ones. Remember: It's never too late to reach out.

Reflections

Think Positively

Finally, brethren, whatever is true, whatever is honorable,
whatever is right, whatever is pure, whatever is lovely,
whatever is of good repute, if there is any excellence
and if anything worthy of praise, let your mind
dwell on these things.

—PHILIPPIANS 4:8

An old Chinese proverb states, "What we think we are." That is so true. Our thought processes determine who we are. If we think lustful thoughts, we become lustful. If thoughts of anger enter our minds, we become angry. What we think is what we begin to feel. Anger, stress, lust, bitterness, and unhappiness have a way of weaseling into our minds and creating a pattern of negativity. We increase our stress and frustration with life when we constantly dialog with ourselves by saying: "I hate my job," "I don't like Mary," "This place is always a mess," "I hate being married," "No one ever helps me with the chores," and "This job is lousy."

If we continue in this mental conversation, we'll begin to internalize these negative beliefs, which is very destructive to our lives.

In order to nip these attacks in the bud, we have to pursue the thoughts of today's Scripture. We must be willing to choose which road we will travel—one that spirals downward or one that spirals upward into a more healthy environment. Paul tells us to think on things that are:

- honorable
- right
- pure
- lovely
- good repute
- whatever is excellent and worthy of praise

This is certainly contrary to what the world, with its immorality, tells us to do. We must make a conscious effort to think in these godly terms. When we do, our whole world will change. These thoughts will give us a new criteria for what we read, view, listen, eat, and think. We will find much riches and the stresses of life will be greatly reduced.

Prayer   *Father God, You have given me only one life to live, and I certainly want it to reflect my love for You. Give me the strength to make the proper choices for my mind, body, and soul. I do want to travel the road less traveled—the road to You. Amen.*

Action   Evaluate what you read, watch, listen to, and eat. What changes need to be made?

Reflections

Treasure Life

*I came that they might have life, and might
have it abundantly.*

—JOHN 10:10

During my recent bout with sickness I have again renewed my zeal to treasure life. As I sit in the doctor's office to receive my chemotherapy treatment every 21 days, I see so many people—some young, some old—who are gravely ill with various forms of cancer. As I leave after my two-and-a-half hour treatment I can truly be grateful for my life. Each morning as I wake there is a new freshness to the day, and each evening as I put my head on the pillow I am so grateful to God for His goodness to me.

The other day my daughter, Jenny, shared with me something that I wasn't even aware of. She stated, "Mom, you and Dad have always used the phrase 'how blessed and thankful we are for where we are in life.' But Mom, it wasn't always good news. Yet you both have been so great about saying how well God provides. In the future my own family is going to be more verbal with the terms *blessed* and *thankful*. Thanks, Mom, for showing me how to have more gratitude." What a joy to receive such a comment from my daughter.

I truly believe we are to treasure life to the fullest. Too often we take this incredible gift of life too much for granted. Appreciation for everything—minor and major events—puts things in perspective and allows us to live a more abundant life. When we feel grateful it affects our whole being. All the trivial issues seems to fall away—and I've discovered that often there's a laugh at the end of the rainbow!

Prayer   Father God, thank You for a treasured life. I love life and want to live it more abundantly. You have given me a grateful heart, and I want to lift up others with this attitude. Amen.

Action   Do something today that reflects your love for your treasured life. Discover the joy of living life abundantly.

Reflections

Let Your Child Be Your Teacher

Behold, children are a gift of the LORD;
the fruit of the womb is a reward.

—PSALM 127:3

We so often think that we are to be our children's teachers, but in reality they can also be our teachers. As our children respond to us in verbal, as well as nonverbal, fashion they often are not very kind with their rebuttals. Often as we walk away from a meeting with our children (no matter what age they are), we feel less confident and more vulnerable than we did before the encounter. My children taught me much about patience, how to handle confrontation, unconditional love, respect, problem solving, rejection, and the ever-changing aspects of life.

Amid your child-rearing frustrations, take on the attitude that your children are actually teaching you some very valuable facets of character development. Rather than becoming upset with their uncooperative behavior, ask God, "What are You trying to teach me in this situation?" Take these opportunities to discover important insights into life. When you begin to look upon your children as your teachers, you won't become nearly as irritated by their behaviors and responses.

As your children begin to see how you respond to them, they will be more willing to improve their communication with you. They have observed that you are a better listener, and that you aren't as reactionary as you have been in the past.

Try this strategy the next time you start to become defensive after one of your children's remarks. Instead, ask, "What can I learn from this situation?" God may be talking to you through your children.

Prayer Father God, may I be willing to learn from the various situations of life. I know You can use my children to teach me. I look forward to learning whatever I can from them. Amen.

Action The next time your child makes you uptight, ask yourself, "Lord, what are You trying to teach me through my children?"

Reflections

☐ ☐ ☐

Symbols of Worship

*Nor do men light a lamp, and put it under the
peck-measure, but on the lampstand; and it
gives light to all who are in the house.*

—MATTHEW 5:15

Have you ever wondered about the various symbols that make up our celebrations of Easter, Thanksgiving, and Christmas? Well, throughout Scripture there are many symbols of worship. An understanding of these symbols will have great significance to our understanding of Scripture and our Christian walk.

The Lion symbolized royalty in ancient Israel. It came to represent the royal line of King David, who came from the tribe of Judah. It also has been associated with justice, strength, and courage. In the New Testament, a fierce lion symbolizes the antichrist and Satan (1 Peter 5:8). One of the titles of Christ is "the Lion of the tribe of Judah" (Revelation 5:5).

The Tabernacle was the Israelites' portable sanctuary for the Ark of the Covenant and the presence of the Lord. In addition to symbolizing holiness (Psalm 15:1), the tabernacle showed that God desired to live among His people.

Bells have been used in worship since the development of Hebrew liturgy (Exodus 28:33,34). The Orthodox church uses bells to mark various points in the liturgy.

The Ark of the Covenant was a physical symbol of God's presence among the Israelites. The Ark bore witness to the covenant between God and His people.

The Rock has been used to represent several different concepts in Scripture. In the Old Testament it symbolizes God's supporting strength and security (1 Samuel 2:2; Psalm 18:2). In the New Testament the rock represents a firm foundation of belief (Luke 6:47,48).

Stars often symbolize countless numbers in the Bible (Genesis 15:5; 22:17). The star is one of the symbols of Christ (Numbers 24:17).

The Aureole [radiant light] symbolizes God's glory and divine light. This image may have developed from the Bible's reference to God's glory as a bright, firelike light (Deuteronomy 33:2; Ezekiel 1:26-28).

The Gate [or portal] in Hebrew and Christian symbolism...signifies entry into an area of great importance....An open gate welcomes the Lord to enter a place (Psalm 24:7). [We are to enter into relationship with the Lord as sheep of His pasture (Psalm 100:4).] Heaven and God's Kingdom are said to have gates (Matthew 7:13). Jesus referred to himself as the gate [door] to salvation (John 10:9).

The Crown symbolizes sovereignty, honor, victory, and praise. Crowns were given to signify royalty and position (2 Kings 11:12; Zechariah 6:11). It was often given to signify that the one who wore it possessed authority and power (Revelation 6:2). We are also a crown of beauty in God's hands (Isaiah 62:3). Jesus was mocked by being forced to wear a crown of thorns (Matthew 27:29).

The Bronze Laver, or washbasin, was placed between the tabernacle and the altar for the priests' cere- monial cleansing (Exodus 30:17-21). The concept of cleansing has carried over into Christianity signifying purity and innocence (John 13:4-11). Pilate washed his hands at Christ's trial to show that the judgment was not his choice—Christ's blood would not be on his hands (Matthew 27:24). Believers are also cleansed by Christ's sacrifice (Hebrews 10:22).

The Altar is a raised area used for sacrifice and sacred ritual. The Hebrew word *altar* literally means "a place of sacrifice." In Christian liturgy the altar symbolizes the table of the Last Supper, which represents the body and blood of Christ.

The Lampstand symbolizes the light of God. The Lord instructed Moses to fashion a lampstand for the tabernacle (Exodus 25:31-40). This lampstand had six branches and a center stem. This came to symbolize God's chosen land (Israel) and inhabit- ants. Jesus told his followers to place the light of their good deeds on a stand for all to see so that they will praise God (Matthew 5:15,16).[15]

Prayer   *Father God, there are words in the Bible that symbolize more than I sometimes know. I want to understand. Let my mind be willing to take the time to research the background of these various symbols of worship so I can get Your whole message and more accurately apply Your instructions. Amen.*

Action   Sing the children's Sunday school song "This Little Light of Mine," remembering that we are God's light among people.

Reflections

---

*God has entrusted us
with family and friends and charged us
with living in a way that helps them
draw closer to Him.*

—EMILIE BARNES

A Home
Needs Care

Older women likewise are to be reverent in their behavior,
not malicious gossips...teaching what is good, that
they may encourage the young women to love
their husbands, to love their children, to be
sensible, pure, workers at home, kind . . .

—TITUS 2:3-5

One morning a very distraught lady called me. She was crying and almost hysterical. I could hardly understand what she was attempting to tell me, but after a few moments of consoling she settled down so we could have a meaningful conversation. The bottom line was that she hadn't learned one of the basic truths of being a mom. She expressed her main problem: "Emilie, I do everything you say to do in your books—and after about six weeks everything is a mess again. What am I doing wrong?" I began to chuckle inside, not letting her know of my humor. You see, we all have this problem with our homes. We want to fix them up and have them stay that way all of our lives. Once we begin to realize that a home is similar to the Golden Gate Bridge we will be much happier. Let me explain.

Bob and I were returning back home from Northern California when our route took us over this giant bridge. As we drove across the spans of steel, Bob told me a story about how workers no sooner get finished chipping away the rust and painting this majestic engineering feat then they have to start all over again and do the same thing. Their work is never done. As homemakers, neither is our work ever done. Until we reconcile ourselves with this fact we will always be stressed out and perhaps angry that all our work seems for naught.

We can get overwhelmed with taking care of our homes because there is always something needing repaired, replaced, painted, or fixed. We will be much happier when we realize that our homes are in process; our homes are where families live and grow. Hang in there and be flexible.

Prayer   Father God, let me relax in my home. I don't want to get stressed out because there is so much that continually needs to be done. Let me realize that that's life. My home is not my enemy but my friend. Thank You for giving to me a home and the family that lives in it. I really appreciate how You've blessed me. You are so generous with Your gifts. Amen.

Action   As you do the dishes for the third time today, be grateful that you have dishes to wash.

Reflections

Why Is God Worthy of Worship?

[God] has made everything appropriate in its time.
He has also set eternity in their heart, yet so that man
will not find out the work which God has done from
the beginning even to the end.

—ECCLESIASTES 3:11

God has given us an eternal perspective so that we can look beyond the routines of life. Nevertheless, He has not revealed all of life's mysteries. When we're feeling down or going through difficult times, two of our major questions of life are, "Why is this happening? Is God worthy of worship?" Mankind has been asking this basic question throughout history. Is it because God works out every detail of our lives? Or because the good guys always win? Is it because He answers the big and difficult questions of life?

If we went to the book of Ecclesiastes and addressed this question to the "teacher," he would say that "God is worthy of worship simply because He is God." God doesn't promise only good things will happen to the believer. Even when life is filled with pain, heartache, and uncertainty God still remains worthy. Even in hard times we must decide if we will "fear God and obey His commands" (Ecclesiastes 12:13). The writer of this great book of the Bible asserts that even though life sometimes seems meaningless it has its satisfactions:

- There is strength and comfort in human companionship (4:9-12).
- Knowing God puts things in perspective (2:24,25).
- Satisfaction with our work is His gift to us (3:13).
- All our deeds are in God's hands (9:1).

Even with his great wisdom, the "teacher" (Solomon) could not figure out all the mysteries of life. Life has its unanswerable questions—and even some contradictions—but we face them knowing that Jesus has already overcome them, giving us hope. God truly is worthy of our worship.

Prayer   Father God, I know it's not very spiritual when I question Your greatness. Thank You for being so gracious and for reminding me that You are always present even when I feel alone. I stand assured that You will never leave me. Amen.

Action   Do you feel alone? If so, let today's reading reassure you that God is present.

Reflections

Never-Ending Desires

I have learned to be content in whatever
circumstances I am.

—Philippians 4:11

We don't happen to live in a society that puts a lid on anything, let alone on our desires. As a capitalistic and consuming society we strive upward to the next level of prosperity: bigger apartments or houses, luxury cars, the next raise, fancier vacations, and more expensive toys. The echo of success says that our happiness depends upon possessions that show those around us that we have succeeded in the business arena.

In and of themselves, there is nothing wrong with owning things. When we work hard there should be rewards at the end of the rainbow; however, we have to be careful to make sure we aren't blinded by our drive to acquire these medals we struggle so hard to attain.

Bob and I have learned to put a limit on our desires. As a couple we have said this is where we stop. We don't need any bigger or better trophies to make us happy and to give life more meaning.

When a person or family puts a ceiling on their desires they, in essence, are announcing to themselves and to the ones around them that they can be happy in the present.

In today's Scripture, Paul is letting us know that

contentment for the now is what's important—not the desires for the future. One definition of contentment is "self-sufficiency independent of external circumstances." We need to train ourselves to verbalize and live out "more isn't always better" instead of "more is going to make me happier." A ceiling on our desires will certainly cut out much of the stress that accompanies accumulating material rewards.

Prayer   *Father God, I'm really tired of gathering things in my life in order to be happy. Thank You for helping me realize that a ceiling on desires is very attainable, and that this contentment will give me real joy. I want to learn to appreciate the now. Amen.*

Action   Come together as a family and discuss the idea of putting a ceiling on your desires.

Reflections

□ □ □

Family Worship

And while they were eating, Jesus took some bread, and after a blessing, He broke it and gave it to the disciples, and said, "Take, eat; this is My body."

—MATTHEW 26:26

here is one practice which any family can maintain and that is the practice of a time of worship at each family meal. Nearly all families are together for at least one meal a day and, in any case, should sacrifice much else to make this possible. *The table is really the family altar!* Here, those of all ages come together and help to sustain both their physical and their spiritual existence. If a sacrament is "an actual conveyance of the spiritual meaning and power by a material process," then the family meal can be a sacrament. It entwines the material and the spiritual in a remarkable way. The food, in and of itself, is purely physical, but it represents human service in its use. Here, at one common table, is the father who has earned, the mother who has prepared or planned, and the children who share, according to need, whatever their antecedent participation may have been.

When we realize how deeply a meal together can be a spiritual and regenerating experience, we can understand something of why our Lord, when he broke bread with his little company toward the end of their earthly fellowship told them, as often as they did it, to remember him. We, too, seek to be members of his sacred fellowship, and irrespective of what we do about the Eucharist, there is no reason why each family meal should not take on something of the character of a time of memory and hope.[16]

—*Elton Trueblood*

"Do this in remembrance of Me" is etched on communion tables all over the world. May we, as family members, take this command and incorporate it into our homes on a daily basis.

Prayer   *Father God, may our family be a family that lives out Your command, "Do this in remembrance of Me." Our dinner table can be an altar in which we give back to You our thankfulness for all You have done for us. Amen.*

Action   Thank God for your food at dinnertime.

Reflections

□ □ □

Birthdays Aren't So Bad

But let each one examine his own work, and then
he will have reason for boasting in regard to himself alone,
and not in regard to another.

—GALATIANS 6:4

We often stand before ourselves on each anniversary of our birth and make comparisons of what we are doing differently than we did in previous years. As we get older we have a tendency to compare back to the "good old days" of our youth or to one of our friends who seem to be surviving the times better than we are.

I had the privilege of knowing June Masters Bacher when she, too, was an author for Harvest House Publishers. What a delightful woman. I had several opportunities to have a meal with her when we met together at the annual Christian Booksellers' Convention. Over one of our meals we talked about birthdays and how traumatic they can be in one's life. June shared with me a story about a friend of her mother's who had a thing about birthdays. I asked her to write it down for me so I could share it with other ladies.

My mother's friend had a thing about birthdays. She overcame it at 65.

151

It rained on Jo's birthday. "That figures," she said. "Gray month. Gray hair. Gray mood." She inspected herself from all angles looking for a bigger bulge or a new liver spot. Always bad, this one was the worst of all—a time (she said) when husbands became interesting "older men" and wives became dull "elderly women."

"Wanting to punish myself," she remembers, "I looked in my scrapbook at the list of advantages of being 21. A glorious day!"

She could vote, date, marry, seek a career, choose her own clothes, travel, live where she wished, read what she chose, forget school routine for a time and *enjoy her freedom!* So?

"That one did it," Jo admitted. "When had I ever been as free as now?" And that was when the dear lady began her list of advantages of turning 65.

Ah yes, she could draw Social Security, ride the city bus free, visit city parks without paying for admission, take adult education courses free, collect Medicare, serve as the sage whose ideas were considered wise and whose services were valuable. There was nothing, in fact, in the first list Jo was unable to do or had not done already. There were countless things she could do now but not then. "Why, I'm a liberated woman!" she cried in discovery.

It is good to pause and count our blessings at every birthday. They pile up with the years. God is changeless. He has work for us here and each milestone shows that He chose to have us remain to give Him a hand. Resolve this year to enjoy your new freedom. Ask God how you can make it count.

Prayer   Father God, thank You for my life and for Your care and provision. Every birthday is a blessing. They bring new opportunities to enjoy my freedom and relish the time You have given me. Amen.

Action   Ask God to show you how to make this next year count for His glory.

Reflections

The measure of a happy life is not from the fewer or more suns to behold, the fewer or more breaths we draw, or meals we repeat, but from having once lived well, acted our part handsomely, and made our exit cheerfully.

—LORD SHAFTESBURY

How many hearts are broken,
How many friends are lost
By some unkind word spoken
Before we count the cost!
But a word or deed of kindness
Will repay a hundredfold,
For it echoes again in the heart of men
And carries a joy untold.

—C.A. LUFBURROW

☐ ☐ ☐

Establishing Balance in Your Home

*Let no unwholesome word proceed from your mouth,
but only such a word as is good for edification according to
the need of the moment, that it may give
grace to those who hear.*

—EPHESIANS 4:29

As a young bride and mother I began to realize that my home operated smoothly when the emotional tone was well thought out. In the first few years of my marriage I was a reactionary to the stresses of the family. Then I realized a little prearranging gave me a head start to prevent possible sources of stress and conflict. I learned to be proactive.

Bob and I have planned together what tone we want our home to reflect. Both of us liked controlled chaos with interludes of soft sounds, quiet moments, moments for reflection and purpose. We don't like to have mass confusion with everyone running around like chickens with their heads cut off. We expect respect, courtesy, and politeness to be exhibited with an air of calm. We want to respect each other's aloneness if he or she wants or needs space.

Today's Scripture was incorporated into our marriage to give us that emotional climate. We collectively made sure that our conversations were uplifting and in a tone of

155

voice that reflected kindness. Did we slip? Of course, but our idealism soon became part of our reality.

One other feature we tried to incorporate was to keep unnecessary rushing around to a minimum. In today's age it becomes very difficult not to become a taxi for everyone's activities. We were each accountable to one another to ask if we weren't rushing around too much as a family or individual. We each had that permission to ask—and to be accountable to—each other. Even today my adult children will often ask me, "Mom, don't you need to slow down?" And you know, they're generally right on! We all need some yellow lights to remind us to have balance and slow down.

Prayer   Father God, You know I want to have a well-running home with a balance in the emotional tone of my family. I truly want the members of my family to find home a place for stillness, revitalizing, stability, and edification. Give me ways to incorporate these characteristics into my home. Amen.

Action   Turn off the TV during evening meals, and play soft background music during your time of togetherness.

Reflections

You Can Touch Stars

*Forgetting what lies behind and reaching forward to
what lies ahead, I press on toward the goal for the
prize of the upward call of God in Christ Jesus.*

—PHILIPPIANS 3:13,14

*S*tars have long been symbols of the unattainable. They should not be so. For although our physical hands cannot reach them, we can touch them in other ways. Let stars stand for those things which are ideal and radiant in life; if we seek sincerely and strive hard enough, it is not impossible to reach them, even though the goals seem distant at the onset. And how often do we touch stars when we find them close by in the shining lives of great souls, in the sparkling universe of humanity around us?

—*Esther Baldwin York*

Have you ever considered that you are a star people can touch? Does your life light up the room when you enter? Do your children and grandchildren reflect back to you the love you give them? Do the elderly say you make a difference in their lives? Yes, you can become a star in so many areas of life if you will only think in the larger terms of life.

We each have 24 hours a day and seven days to the week. What are you going to do with yours? All of the great conquests of life have started as a little idea in someone's head. It's what is done with that idea that counts.

What are the deepest dreams you have? Maybe writing a song, starting a business, authoring a book, helping children, creating a new recipe? Reach out today and plan how you are going to energize that thought into reality. Don't let it fall to the ground and perish. Nurture and water it until the sunlight makes it grow.

We are elevated by our constant aspirations. Scripture says that without a vision a nation will perish—and so will we. As Christians we either grow or we begin to slide backward. No one advances by accident; all achievements are reached by a dream.

Daniel H. Burnham once said, "Make no little plans, they have no magic to stir men's blood...make big plans, aim high in hope and work."

Prayer　　　*Father God, I love to look into the vastness of space to see the twinkle of Your stars. May I be able to reach out and touch their light beams. Thank You for putting aspirations in my mind. May I develop them to your glory. Amen.*

Action　　　Write down three dreams you have. What are you going to do with them?

Reflections

This Little Light of Mine

❧❦❧

No one, after lighting a lamp, puts it away in a cellar,
nor under a peck-measure, but on the lampstand, in order
that those who enter may see the light.

—LUKE 11:33

*I*n a certain mountain village in Europe several centuries ago (so the story goes), a nobleman wondered what legacy to leave his townspeople. At last he decided to build them a church.

Nobody saw the complete plans until the church was finished. When the people gathered, they marveled at its beauty. But one noticed an incompleteness.

"Where are the lamps?" he asked. "How will the church be lighted?"

The nobleman smiled. Then he gave each family a lamp. "Each time you are here, the area in which you sit will be lighted. But when you are not here, some part of God's house will be dark."

Today we live in a world of darkness, dim paths on which even our secular problem-solvers are beginning to stumble. In spite of our social conscience, all around us is evidence of ignorance, illiteracy, and wicked imaginings.

Romans 2:19 tells us that we, as Christians, are "a light to those who are in darkness."

But the world is so big, and our lamps are so small. Yes—but we can light some small part of each day. Look to the star-struck heavens. How small each star looks in the distance. Yet, put together, those tiny jewels can light the darkest night. Each of us is a star (or a lamp, if you will). We can make this world a brighter place. It all begins with the desire expressed in Michelangelo's prayer: "God, grant me the desire always to desire to be more than I can ever accomplish."

Prayer Father God, You are my lamp, and may I always reflect Your love to the dark world as I pass through. I trust my life is a radiant light that other people might be guided to You. I want to keep my lamp full of oil so my path will be lit by Your glow. Amen.

Action Light your lamp. Let God send you in a new direction today. Meet someone at the crossroads of his or her life and share your light.

Reflections

Three Gates

My lips will not speak wickedness,
and my tongue will utter no deceit. . . . I
will not deny my integrity. I will maintain
my righteousness; . . . my conscience
will not reproach me.

—JOB 27:4-6

*A*n old Arabian proverb states:

If you are tempted to reveal a tale someone has told about another, make it pass, before you speak, three gates of gold. These narrow gates: First, "Is it true?" Then "Is it needful?" In your mind give truthful answers. And the next is last and narrowest, "Is it kind?" And if to reach your lips at last it passes through these gateways three, then you may tell the tale, nor fear what the result of speech may be.

If all of us could remember these three gates we would have more love in our relationships and our friendships would be everlasting. Think back over the years and recall situations where a story was told by you that would not pass the three-gate test. How did it affect your friendship? Scripture is very clear when it tells us not to speak unwholesome words from our mouths. Our utterances should be edifying (uplifting) and give grace to the hearer. As Florence Littauer says, "Our words are to be given as a silver box with a bow on it."

Wouldn't it be great if our speech would always be as a gift wrapped from our favorite department store? A gift so wonderful we can hardly wait for the recipients to unwrap it? Evaluate your style of speech to see if what you say will pass the gate test. If not, be more careful.

Prayer *Father God, may I always be sensitive to the stories I pass on to a listener. Help me to make sure my words are true, needful, and kind. I want my speech to be pleasing to Your name. Amen.*

Action Today use the three-gate test for all your conversations.

Reflections

☐ ☐ ☐

Learn to Live in the Present

Do not be anxious for your life, as to what you shall eat,
or what you shall drink; nor for your body, as
to what you shall put on. Is not life more than
food, and the body than clothing?

—MATTHEW 6:25

As I've observed my five grandchildren over the years, one thing stands out very vividly—their ability to live and enjoy the moment. I have become so interested in how they can take the "now" and make it a present. As I get older, I'm trying to forget about what happened yesterday and what might happen tomorrow and just experience the fullness of today.

In order to capture the essence of the present, we need to give less attention to worries, mistakes, what's going wrong, general concerns, things to get done, the past, the future, and the undone. "Today I will only think about today. No regrets for the past or future maybes." When you do this all your focus is on the now—you can smile, laugh, pray, think, and enjoy what the moment brings. At the beach, in the mountains, cleaning house, cooking a meal, and playing in the sandbox with a grandchild—that's where I find purpose and enjoyment. Often our anxieties

163

are about situations we have no control over. I tell the ladies at my seminars that 85 percent of the things we worry about never happen. So why spend all that negative energy on something that probably won't occur?

My friend Florence Littauer has often encouraged her readers to learn to live life on purpose. We are to stop and smell the roses, hear the train whistle, see the puffy clouds in the sky, and enjoy life as God has given it to us. When we begin to see and experience the minute, we will begin to see the grandeur of God and His vastness. As we focus on the present we will spend less time worrying about tomorrow. Become as a little child and enjoy now....

Prayer   Father God, block out yesterday, and don't let me try to glimpse tomorrow. I want to make a present out of today. I truly want to observe all that You have given me now. May today be the greatest day of my life because I've enjoyed every moment in it. Amen.

Action   Buy yourself your favorite ice cream or yogurt and enjoy every morsel of the sweet taste.

Reflections

Character Does Count

*You should remember that though another may have more money,
beauty, and brains than you, yet when it comes to the rarer
spiritual values such as charity, self-sacrifice, honor, nobility
of heart, you have an equal chance with everyone to
be the most beloved and honored of all people.*

—ARCHIBALD RUTLEDGE

*D*oes character matter? One side of the fence argues that as long as a person does the job he is supposed to do it really doesn't matter what he does on his own. The other side defends the Judeo-Christian position that character is the alpha and omega. What else is there if not character?

Many times we think character only belongs to the masculine gender; that it's something women don't have to wrestle with. However, we must come face-to-face with this issue. We are the ones who rock the cradles of the future leaders of our country. We are the inspiration for those who live in our homes, eat our meals, learn our prayers, and nestle in our beds at night.

One of the disturbing trends that I see as I travel this country is how the young women of our culture have taken on the characteristics that have historically been held been by men. I see them smoking, cussing, telling off-color jokes, seducing young men, and drinking to intoxication. They have lost the elements we have known as being soft and tender. God did not mean for women to be hard and manlike. Woman was to be a helper not a confronter. The capable wife of Proverbs 31 depicts the various character traits of an excellent wife. The key to her beautiful character is her spiritual life. She is a godly woman who fears the Lord.

Prayer   Father God, as I approach Your throne I bow humbly before You. May I be a teacher of character to my children and their children. May they look upon my life as an example of what You want a godly woman to reflect. I want to be a character role-model for You. Praise Your name! Amen.

Action   Read Proverbs 30:10-31.

Reflections

□ □ □

A Woman in the Mirror

For that which I am doing, I do not understand;
for I am not practicing what I would like to do,
but I am doing the very thing I hate.

—ROMANS 7:15

A wise woman once said, "The person I have the most trouble with is the person I see in my mirror every day."

Jeanette Lockerbie has shared some thoughts regarding this verse of Scripture:

> What Christian has not sincerely grieved over her own spiritual shortcomings, over doing those things I ought not to have done and leaving undone those things I ought to have done.
>
> No follower of Christ was ever more acutely conscious of this very trait and tendency than the apostle Paul. We might take comfort from that thought, but to allow ourselves to be trapped in Satan's snare by wallowing in despair is to disparage the limitless, liberating grace of God.
>
> Let us not linger in the valley of spiritual desolation. There is a way to get rid of "troublesome you" or "troublesome me." The cry, "Who will rescue me?" echoes to the very throne of God. The reply,

167

ringing with triumphant deliverance and assurance, echoes to our very ears.

There is therefore now no condemnation for those who are in Christ Jesus (Romans 8:1).

When I look into that dimly lit mirror each day I can stand assured that I am a child of God, and with all that He has done for me I can step out and exercise the power He has given on the cross. All my sins are forgiven and there is no condemnation that can separate me from His eternal love. Even though I am not perfect in myself, I take on Jesus' righteousness and am found to be spotless before God. Praise the Lord for that assurance!

Prayer   *Father God, I am so glad that what I see in the mirror is not all I am. Your perfect sacrifice has made me whole. My mirror reflects Your goodness and assures me that I am Your child. Amen.*

Action   Look in a mirror and say these words: "There is therefore no condemnation for those who are in Christ Jesus."

Reflections

☐ ☐ ☐

Don't Answer the Phone

Your success as family, our success as society,
depends not on what happens in the White House,
but on what happens in your house.

—BARBARA BUSH

*T*here are only a few things in life that can truly be controlled by us. One of these is what we do when the phone rings. You have the power to control this intrusion in your family's life. As we look around, we see we have become slaves to the telephone. The other day I was dining in a fine restaurant with a friend when it was disturbed by a very boisterous gentleman on a cell phone. He made everyone around his table aware that he was far more important than we were because he had no consideration for our being deprived of an enjoyable experience at lunch.

How many times has the phone rung while your family was having a quiet meal together? Everyone looks anxiously at each other, wondering who will bolt to the phone to see who's there. Don't answer the phone at mealtime unless you are expecting an emergency phone call. Let the family know that they are much more important than the unknown person at the other end of the line. Yes, there are certain situations when you don't need to answer the phone.

I've been known to switch off the ringer on the phone during important times of the evening. This way we don't hear the rings and aren't inclined to interrupt our evening time together. The answering machine or voice mail will pick up the message, and we can reply at a more convenient time.

Certainly there will be times when we need to answer the phone, but *you* decide when. Don't let others control your life and alter your scheduled activities. Ask yourself: "Is my life going to be made easier or will there be more stress by answering the phone whenever it rings?" You have the power to decide.

Prayer   Father God, prevent me from automatically being a slave to the phone. Empower me to make that decision. There are times and occasions when I want to say no. Who says that all calls must be answered personally right away! Amen.

Action   For one week don't answer the telephone during dinnertime. You'll discover a more peaceful family time together.

Reflections

Grant Me Success Today

O LORD, the God of my master Abraham, please
grant me success today, and show
lovingkindness to my master Abraham.

—GENESIS 24:12

All human beings have failings, all human beings have needs and temptations and stresses. Men and women who live together through long years get to know one another's failings; but they also come to know what is worthy of respect and admonition in those they live with and in themselves. If at the end one can say, "This man used to the limit the powers that God granted him and he was worthy of love and respect and of the sacrifices many people made in order that he might achieve what he deemed to be his task"; then, that life has been lived well and there are no regrets.

—*Eleanor Roosevelt*

Recently at the church I attend, one of our missionaries shared that 50 people were necessary to back up each missionary in the field. In missions, and many other endeavors, people must be able to enlist others to make

171

sacrifices for the goals of the cause. I'm always amazed that others will make great sacrifice for someone else's work.

As a writer, I'm always thrilled to see how my publisher puts my latest book together. I stand amazed when I begin to realize how many people it takes to make a book: editors, typesetters, proofreaders, printers, binders, publicity and marketing staff, sales personnel, bookstore owners and their sales staff, and finally the consumer who ultimately purchases the book. People give me all the credit for the book when in reality I'm just one small part of the process even though my name is on the cover. It takes time and effort by a lot of people to bring success to an individual.

According to the great actress Helen Hayes, there is a big difference between achievement and success. She said that "achievement is the knowledge that you have studied and worked hard and done the best that is in you. Success is being praised by others, and that's nice too but not as important or satisfying. Always aim for achievement and forget about success."

I have found that as we strive to achieve in our chosen fields, success will follow. There are no short-cuts to the top. Notice from today's verse that the writer was not only praying for his own success, but that God would show lovingkindness to his master. May those who sacrifice be also blessed.

Prayer   Father God, may those who help me be successful also receive lovingkindness from You. I appreciate all You have done to help me along the way. May I never forget those who have lifted me up. Amen.

Action   Do something today that will help you advance in your chosen field: read a book, take a class, attend a seminar, or teach what you know to someone else.

Reflections

The Haven of Home

By wisdom a house is built, and by understanding
it is established; and by knowledge the rooms are filled
with all precious and pleasant riches.

—PROVERBS 24:3,4

home is a man's castle. It is a place where weary and tired journeyers find peace and quiet after a long day of travels. We don't protect this structure because we are selfish, but because we don't want the craziness of the world to enter into the walls and destroy the restorations that a calm and peaceful home provides for those who live inside and cross its moat. It is one of the only places left where a man and his family can turn away the cares of the world. In my books *Spirit of Loveliness* and *Welcome Home*, I help readers discover how they can set the tone for the family as they come back home each day. My husband, Bob, used to tell me he couldn't wait to get home in the evening because it held so much comfort within its walls.

The home is where your privacy can be protected; you can set the atmosphere and interactions any way you want, including:

- keeping a quiet spirit that's reflected in the home
- talking politely at all times
- using courteous manners

- having soothing music playing
- choosing not to answer the phone while enjoying meals or special times together

You and your family need to decide how your quiet times will be protected. We have a saying around our home, "Say *no* to good things, and save your *yeses* for the best." When you enter your home, know that it is yours not someone else's. No matter how small or how large your house might be, let your privacy reign supreme.

Prayer   Father God, let me continue to preserve the privacy of my home. May I take the time to protect what comes into the house so only those things that give peace and tranquility to my family can come in. Make my home a place where the occupants can find freedom from the struggles of the world. Amen.

Action   Get together as a family and discuss ways to make your home a safe haven amid the world's chaos.

Reflections

The Love of God

For God so loved the world, that He gave His only begotten Son, that whoever believes in Him should not perish, but have eternal life.

—JOHN 3:16

Because the cross alone measures "the breadth, and length, and depth, and height" of the love of God, it is beyond the comprehension of man. The love of Christ "passeth knowledge." Its "breadth" is wide enough to comprehend the whole world, including all races. Its "length" reaches down through all ages from the beginning to the end of the reign of sin. Its "depth" reaches down to the lowest deeps of man's degradation and saves even "to the uttermost." Its "height" includes the highest heaven, to which it will eventually lift those who know its power.[17]

—*Taylor G. Bunch*

What greater love could a person exhibit than to lay down his or her life for a friend. Tears come to my eyes as I dwell on the Easter story. The grossness of the pain of crucifixion is beyond my comprehension. I flinch when I envision the hilltop cross that carried my Lord to His death. I am so very appreciative that He would give His own life that I may have eternal life by accepting Him as my Savior. I will never understand this side of heaven, but I do accept His gracious act for my salvation. May God be glorified for giving us a way to have forgiveness of sin.

Prayer   Father God, how can I say thank You for all You've done in my life? I don't know where I would be if You hadn't died on the cross for my sins. You have been the redeemer of my sinful life. Thank You for enduring the pain for my redemption. May I be willing to glorify Your name in everything I do. Amen.

Action   Meet with God today and thank Him for all He's done for you.

Reflections

Eternity is not something that begins after
you are dead. It is going on all the time.
We are in it now.

—CHARLOTTE PERKINS GILMAN

"Mom, I'm Bored!"

All discipline for the moment seems not to be joyful,
but sorrowful; yet to those who have been trained by it,
afterwards it yields the peaceful
fruit of righteousness.

—HEBREWS 12:11

One of the phrases that used to really bug me when the children were at home was, "Mom, I'm bored!" Then I had the responsibility to think of some creative way to entertain them. Wrong! Today's children have had so much over-stimulation by the multiplicity of choices that when there is a quiet moment they find themselves without something to do—so they think they are bored. Over the years I realized there is nothing wrong with "being bored." We don't have to fall into the trap of thinking we must fill every moment with activities. In reality, we don't have "to do"; we have to learn to "be."

Let the children solve their own problems of inactivity. They have to learn to be problem-solvers because you won't always be around to give them suggestions on what to do. However, you can be a model of what to do with those few precious down-times during the day: read a book, listen to good music, write a letter, make a batch of cookies, crawl up on the sofa and take a 20-minute nap.

Don't try to entertain or stimulate your children out of their boredom. It's their responsibility to be creative.

But you can help them understand that an activity won't always solve the boredom problem. There's nothing wrong if we aren't doing something every moment of the day. Time to relax is okay; we all need to learn how to live with it. Teach your kids to take those quiet times as gifts from heaven. Show them how they can use them to recharge their batteries.

Prayer   Father God, thanks for giving me those quiet times during the day—let me teach my children to use these minutes as a time to rest and enjoy life. Let me show them how to create and get the most out of these quiet times. May my family look at boredom as a great opportunity to "be" in Your presence. Amen.

Action   Think of how you can share the joy of down-time when your children come to you next time and say, "Mom, we're bored."

Reflections

□ □ □

Where Do You Find Your Answers?

*For everything created by God is good,
and nothing is to be rejected, if it is received
with gratitude; for it is sanctified by
means of the word of God and prayer.*

—1 TIMOTHY 4:4,5

The media flood us with various sources for answers to life's basic questions. Television pushes late-evening info commercials that promise happiness using their products. The New Age movement floods bookstores with its brand of answers. Movie and TV personalities are on numerous talk shows hawking their latest interests. The newsstands have beautifully designed magazines that encourage you to buy them so you can read their articles that will help you unravel the mysteries of life—so they say.

We all are searching for answers. What about you? Many of us believe the Bible is God's Word to His people. We have found in the Bible the best explanation of our sense of lostness: "For all have sinned and fall short of the glory of God" (Romans 3:23). In like manner we have discovered in God's Word the best solution to the problem: "For God so loved the world, that He gave His only begotten Son, that whoever believes in Him should not perish, but have eternal life" (John 3:16). In fact, we accept His claim to be not only the best solution but the *only* solution: "I am the way, and the truth, and the life; no one comes to the Father but through Me" (John 14:6).

How can we believe the Bible? What can explain such trust in its teachings? A partial explanation can be found by looking at the Bible itself.

Consider its profundity of content. It was written by many people who never knew each other, with rare opportunities to compare notes. It was written over hundreds of years, yet with a single theme and no contradictions.

Think about the miracle of its survival. Never has one book been so physically threatened. Copies of the Bible have been cut to pieces, thrown into the ocean, and burned to ashes. Emperors, kings, and religious leaders tried to destroy it, yet it has multiplied with every assault.

Others have sought to discredit it intellectually. The great French philosopher Voltaire once held a copy of the Bible high and snarled: "In 100 years this book will be of interest only to some antiquarian curiosity seeker." Within 100 years Voltaire's home housed the Genesis Bible Society. From his former home, thousands upon thousands of Bibles were sent all over Europe! At that same time, a complete set of the works of Voltaire sold on the market for 11 cents. In contrast, the British Parliament paid the Czar of Russia $500,000 for the Codex Sinaiticus, a copy of the Bible.

The Word of God introduces us to Jesus Christ who came from heaven to earth to show us what God is like. Because of Christ, we know of God's love for us. Christ became one of us. He hurt, He suffered, He cared. He laughed with those who laughed, and He cried with those who cried. He still does. He died on the cross to pay for your sins and mine. He came out of His grave so that we would not have to stay in ours. He has prepared a place for us to join Him in heaven when our stay on earth is done.

How do we know this is true? The Word of God shares all this and many more thrilling answers. Where do you go for answers? There's no better source of truth than the Bible.

Prayer   *Father God, I don't know where I would be if I didn't have Your Word in my life. My Bible has been my salvation. Whatever I know is from the revelation of Your Scriptures. Your Word lights my pathway when I seem lost. Thank You. Amen.*

Action   Pray to God acknowledging your appreciation to Him for inspiring the writers of the Bible to write down exactly what instructions He wants us to have.

Reflections

We can trust God
because of what He is like,
because of what He has done.
He has shown us who He is
and what His intentions are
toward His children.
By His Word and
by His actions He reveals
His trustworthiness.

—EMILIE BARNES

A Faith Life Requires Training

All things are possible to him who believes.

—MARK 9:23

rs. Charles E. Cowman and her husband served as pioneer missionaries in Japan and China from 1901–1917. She has reflected on how God teaches us the way of faith. It does not come without its price. She reflects,

> The "everything" in this verse does not always come simply for the asking. God is ever seeking to teach us the way of faith, and in our training in the faith life there must be room for the trial of faith, the discipline of faith, the patience of faith, the courage of faith, and often many stages are passed before we really realize what is the end of faith, namely, the victory of faith.
>
> Real moral fiber is developed through discipline of faith. You have made your request of God, but the answer does not come. What are you to do?
>
> Keep on believing God's Word; never be moved away from it by what you see or feel, and thus as you stand steady, enlarged power and experience is

being developed. The fact of looking at the apparent contradiction as to God's Word and being unmoved from your position of faith make you stronger on every other line.

Often God delays purposely, and the delay is just as much an answer to your prayer as is the fulfillment when it comes.

In the lives of all the great Bible characters God worked thus. Abraham, Moses and Elijah were not great in the beginning, but were made great through the discipline of their faith, and only then were they fitted for the positions to which God had called them.

For example, in the case of Joseph whom the Lord was training for the throne of Egypt, it was not the prison life with its hard beds or poor food that tried him, but it was the word God had spoken into his heart in the early years concerning elevation and honor which were greater than his brethren were to receive. It was this which was ever before him, when every step in his career made it seem more and more impossible of fulfillment. These were hours that tried his soul, but [also] hours of spiritual growth and development.

No amount of persecution tries like such experiences as these. When God has spoken to his purpose to do, and yet the days go on and he does not do it, that is truly hard; but it is a discipline of faith that will bring us into a knowledge of God which would otherwise be impossible.[18]

Prayer   *Father God, let me be able to wait quietly for the trial of faith, the discipline of faith, the patience of faith, and the courage of faith. Through all this may I be able to experience the victory of faith. Amen.*

Action   How is God dealing with you regarding the training of faith in your life? Write down this process. Share it with a friend. Thank God for it.

Reflections

No one is so rich that he does not need another's help; no one so poor as not to be useful in some way to his fellow man; and the disposition to ask assistance from others with confidence, and to grant it with kindness, is part of our very nature.

—POPE LEO XIII

I shall not pass this way again;
Then let me now relieve some pain,
Remove some barrier from the road,
Or brighten some one's heavy load.

—EVA ROSE YORK

Give Yourself
a Few Extra Minutes

Finish every day and be done with it. You have done what you could.
Some blunders and absurdities no doubt crept in; forget them as soon
as you can. Tomorrow is a new day; begin it well and serenely, and
with too high a spirit to be cumbered with your old nonsense. This
day is all that is good and fair. It is too dear with its hopes and
invitations, to waste a moment on yesterday.

—RALPH WALDO EMERSON

My Bob has the great virtue of always being on time. Our son, Brad, once asked him, "Dad, aren't you ever late?" His question was a compliment for timeliness.

Being on time is certainly a virtue. We can prioritize our appointments so we aren't stressed trying to get to them. I have found that if I allow myself at least ten extra minutes between activities, I have a greater sense of peace. That last minute push to catch up for that next activity is what can drive us crazy—and it can mean the difference between a good day or a bad day. I tell myself that I'm going to be ten minutes early. That way, I have a few extra minutes to arrive refreshed instead of stressed and haggard. Don't start another activity until you are all-the-way ready for the next appointment.

When we're on time, we will enjoy the day rather than rushing through life helter-skelter.

Prayer   Father God, You know I don't want chaos in my life. I beg of You to help me be ten minutes early for my appointments. I don't like my gut feeling when I'm running late to the next activity. I don't want to be behind. I really want to be early. Amen.

Action   Don't overschedule your activities. Leave a little time between each activity. Allow for some down-time by scheduling breaks.

Reflections

My quiet time is not a gift I give to God; my quiet time is a gift God gives to me.

—AUTHOR UNKNOWN

A Spot That Wouldn't Go Away

*If we confess our sins, He is faithful and righteous to
forgive us our sins and to cleanse us from
all unrighteousness.*

—1 JOHN 1:9

ne day, after a busy day of painting our
wrought-iron fence green, Bob came into
the house to eat lunch. He thought he had
cleaned up adequately, but he missed one spot of green
paint on his right elbow. As he rested his elbow on my
recently cleaned, white, quilted tablecloth, he noticed that
a spot of green paint was transferred from his elbow onto
the tablecloth. Immediately, he knew he was in trouble.
He soaked a rag with paint thinner and used some elbow
grease on the stain, but to no avail. The spot would not
disappear. He tried again and again, but the spot was still
visible.

To this date, the green stain still appears to remind me
that sin is that way in our lives. Once it has tainted my soul,
I can try and try to remove it, but it stays until I go to the
cross and ask for forgiveness from God. Positionally, I know
that Jesus died on the cross for all my sins—past, present,
and future. What a wonderful assurance to know that I
have the best stain remover in the universe with Jesus!

If we still carry the heavy burden of sin around it affects our radiance, confidence, emotional stability, and physical well-being. Much of our dysfunction is because we haven't learned to ask Jesus to carry our sins for us.

If you are one of those people who carry around the heavy load of transgressions, you can be forgiven today. Take on a new life by asking Jesus to come into your life! He will lift from your shoulders the stain of sin that won't go away.

Prayer   *Father God, I ask You to step in and forgive me of all my sins. I'm tired of trying to clean up my life all by myself. I have no more strength left. Send into my life a mentor who will train me to be a woman of God. Amen.*

Action   Make a commitment of Christian faith today. If you're already a believer, seek out someone you can mentor.

Reflections

□ □ □

Amazing Grace

Grow in the grace and knowledge of our
Lord and Savior Jesus Christ. To Him be the glory,
both now and to the day of eternity. Amen.

—2 Peter 3:18

John Newton (1725–1807) called himself a wretch who was lost and blind. As a young boy of 11, he left school to begin the rough life of a seaman. He wound up engaged in the practice of capturing natives from West Africa to be sold as slaves. Through circumstances in his life, and after being inspired by certain readings of godly inspiration, John had a dramatic conversion into a new way of life. At age 39, John Newton became an ordained minister of the Anglican Church in the small village of Olney, England.

One of Newton's songs, "Amazing Grace," is a story of his early life as a sinner and how the grace of God saved him into a life of ministry. Until the time of his death at 82, John Newton never stopped marveling at God's grace for his life. At the end of his life, he is credited as saying with a loud voice, "My memory is nearly gone, but I remember two things: that I am a great sinner; that Christ is a great Savior. That is amazing grace."

Amazing grace! How sweet the sound that saved a wretch like me! I once was lost, but now am found; was blind, but now I see.

191

'Twas grace that taught my heart to fear, and grace my fears relieved; how precious did that grace appear the hour I first believed.

Through many dangers, toils and snares, I have already come; 'tis grace hath brought me safe thus far, and grace will lead me home.

The Lord has promised good to me, His word my hope secures; He will my shield and portion be, as long as life endures.

When we've been there ten thousand years, bright shining as the sun, we've no less days to sing God's praise than when we'd first begun.[19]

The theme throughout Scripture is how wretched we are and how God, through His Son, Jesus, has redeemed us from our sin situation. God is always most gracious in our weakest area of life. Where we work from our strengths, Christ works from our weaknesses. As fellow believers, we can have a great impact on the world when we:

- celebrate grace in our own lives by being willing to share with others how Christ has saved us from a life of sin

- recognize the people who need grace by being an observer of people around us. Every day we meet people who need Jesus

- make grace the style of our lives by having compassion for those who need lifting up

Grace is the style of God's love for mankind. The last verse of the Bible reads, "The grace of the Lord Jesus be with all. Amen" (Revelation 22:21).

Prayer   *Father God, even though I wasn't a slave trader, I was every bit as much a sinner as John Newton. I thank You for reaching down and saving me by Your grace. I certainly didn't deserve it, and my works weren't capable of doing what You did by Your grace. May I always realize that You are a great Savior. Amen.*

Action

Spend some time alone today thinking and praising God for what He has done for you by His grace.

Reflections

---

*I sought to hear the voice of God
And climbed the top most steeple,
But God declared:
"Go down again—
I dwell among the people."*

—LOUIS I. NEWMAN

A house is built of logs and stone,
of tiles and posts and piers;
A home is built of loving deeds
that stand a thousand years.

—VICTOR HUGO

☐ ☐ ☐

Let Your Home Reflect Love

If I am inconsiderate about the comfort of others, or their feelings, or even their little weaknesses; if I am careless about their little hurts and miss opportunities to smooth their way; if I make the sweet running of household wheels more difficult to accomplish, then I know nothing of Calvary's love.

—AMY CARMICHAEL

can't walk in my front door without seeing evidences of love. Everywhere I look I'm reminded that Bob and I have created a home in which you're going to get loved. As you walk up the path to the front door, you see roses, a rose arbor, potted plants with welcome signs everywhere. As you enter, you see uplifting signs of encouragement, pictures hanging that reflect our family values, and a coffee table filled with family pictures dating back five generations. Even though many have passed on, their names are familiar to the grandchildren because we talk of them as if they're still alive.

The furniture says, "Welcome, you can come and sit on me; it's okay if you mess up the pillows." There is an abundance of freshly cut flowers that release sweet-smelling fragrances of nature. In the kitchen all kinds of children's art hang on the front of the refrigerator. The grandchildren love to furnish the latest in their designs for display in our home.

The refrigerator is open for the tiny hands to check out its contents. They can always find the ingredients for their favorite treats. The adults who filter in find fresh drink and soothing music that relaxes stress and tension.

People often comment how relaxed and loved they feel in our home. It's almost impossible not to feel loved when you are in a setting that says "I love you."

Does your home reflect God's love and provision? Is it an oasis of peace?

Prayer   Father God, thank You for showing me how I can show Your love in my home. We don't always have to verbally say "I love you," even though that's important. The nonverbal language is just as effective. Amen.

Action   Do something to your home that says "I love you!"

Reflections

☐ ☐ ☐

Stay Loose

I need to slow down and I'm asking the Lord to help me do it. I want to move slowly enough to be aware of all the joys He has hidden for me. I want to slow down enough to grow as He wants me to grow. I want to be quiet enough to hear His voice. I need His wisdom to know how to spend my time and how to order my days.

—KATHRYN HILLEN

As you know, I'm known for organization, to-do lists, organization charts, appointments, and doing more than one thing at a time, but there are times when you have children at home that you need to stay loose. As most of you have probably already experienced, rigidity can be a negative when raising children. When you have all your i's dotted and your t's crossed, you end up with a lot of disappointments due to false expectations. You start out the day with a full agenda, and soon it's noon and nothing has been checked off your list. Sometimes with children that's the way it goes. Hang loose and keep on plugging away. What doesn't get done today can slide over until tomorrow. Yes, there are times when we must accomplish certain tasks, but in general rigidities cause a lot of stress in our lives.

Usually these rigid agendas prevent you from accomplishments. When you are loose, you can shift gears a lot easier when an emergency arises—and they do.

The dinosaurs became extinct because they couldn't adjust to their environment. Too much inflexibility will also cause us to burn out as wives and moms. Don't let your mind tell you that you are ineffective. Relax and be assured that you're okay as a wife and mom. Try to be less rigid and laugh more.

Prayer   Father God, let me be looser with my daily agendas. I try to give myself a lot of latitude as I help raise my children. Keep the guilt trip out of my mind. With children, I want to concentrate on the now and not on a stuffed-full program each day. Amen.

Action   Work on this mind-set. Stay flexible with today's agenda; go with the flow.

Reflections

Conformed Versus Transformed

*And do not be conformed to this world, but be
transformed by the renewing of your mind, that you may
prove what the will of God is, that which is good
and acceptable and perfect.*

—ROMANS 12:2

ave you ever asked, "What is the will
of God for my life?" I know I have
many times. This question seems like
the biggest mystery of the Christian walk. How do I know
that? Well, I have used this passage as a help to first make
me realize that there is a tremendous battle going on in my
mind between good and evil, right and wrong, godly and
ungodly. This verse is a reminder regarding that battle. I
always want to be in God's will and not my own. I must
open my mind to realize that the world (secular thinking)
is trying to win me over to its side. However, the warning
in Romans is not to be conformed, but to *be transformed* by
the renewing of my mind so that I can:

- know what the will of God is
- learn what is good, acceptable, and perfect

A companion verse to help me in this transformation of the mind is found in Philippians 4:8, which reads: "Finally brethren, whatever is true, whatever is honorable, whatever is right, whatever is pure, whatever is lovely, whatever is of good repute, if there is any excellence and if anything worthy of praise, let your mind dwell on these things."

I can assure you that if you use these two verses, and if you search the Scriptures, your mind will be transformed and you'll know what the will of God is for your life. Don't forget to talk to well-respected Christians and pastors, too. Their insights can be very helpful. Formulate your direction and move out. Because you are earnestly seeking God's will, if you are going in the wrong direction, He will correct your course.

Prayer *Father God, I appreciate all the various verses of Scripture You put into my heart so I can be drawing closer to You all the time. I'm glad You have put in my heart a desire for goodness. Amen.*

Action Write down three things you can do to transform your life in a godly direction. Work on incorporating these into your life.

Reflections

□ □ □

Keep Your Joy Alive

Therefore you too now have sorrow;
but I will see you again, and your heart will rejoice,
and no one takes your joy away from you.

—JOHN 16:22

Isn't life glorious! Isn't it grand!
Here—take it—hold it tightly in your hand;
Squeeze every drop of it into your soul,
Drink of the joy of it, sun-sweet and whole!
Laugh with the love of it, burst into song!
Scatter its richness as you stride along!
Isn't life splendid—and isn't it great
We can always start living—it's never too late!

—*Helen Louise Marshall*

Joy will always follow sorrow. I've met so
many women who are right in the middle
of sorrow—a death, a separation, a divorce,
a serious health problem, teenage children that are rebel-
ling, financial difficulties, an unbelieving mate. The list
goes on and on.

Each of us at one time or the other has been in deep
sorrow. Sometimes it seems like a smile will never appear

201

on our faces because the burden is so heavy and the load is so great.

Between my illness and the heartache of my daughter's troubled marriage, my heart has been so heavy. The tears of sorrow stream down my face and soak my pillow. As I begin to pray for my situation, I plead to God to "restore to me the joy of Thy salvation" (Psalm 51:12). A friend will call, I will receive a note through the mail, or a fax with a verse of Scripture or poem will appear. The load becomes lighter and I can pray to God to continue my joy even during my time of trouble.

In my Bible I have a card that reads, "Don't doubt in the morning what God has promised you in the night." Don't let anyone or anything take away your joy. It is yours to have and to hold.

Prayer   *Father God, help me see Your beauty all around me. May my thankfulness of joy spill over from a cupful of "thank Yous." Joy is a decision on my part, and I'm committed that no one can take that away from me. Amen.*

Action   Call a friend today who might need a reminder that God loves him or her—and so do you.

Reflections

Do I Need to Join a Church?

You are Peter, and upon this rock I will build
My church; and the gates of Hades shall
not overpower it.

—MATTHEW 16:18

The name of Peter means "rock," or "rockman" in the Greek. Jesus did not say, "Upon you, Peter" or "Upon your successors," but "Upon this rock"—upon this divine revelation and profession of faith in Christ. "I will build" shows that the formation of the church was still in the future. It began on the day of Pentecost (read Acts 2).

Every week, millions of people gather in church buildings all over the world. Many other millions choose not to attend for one reason or another. Some feel that the church has very little meaning for their lives. Still others see the church as conflicting with the way they want to live.

How do you see the church? How do you think of it? One of the joys of the Christian life is that of being an active member of a church. The apostle Paul wrote to the members in the church at Philippi: "I thank my God in all my remembrance of you" (Philippians 1:3). Even while in chains in a Roman prison, every thought of the church brought joy to Paul's heart. Every church member should

204 • *Meet Me Where I Am, Lord*

feel that way about his or her church. If you are considering joining a church, you should have a feeling of joy about the church you choose.

Often we think of the church as the building in which we meet to worship or study. However, the church is not the building; it's the people who make up its membership. Even when they are scattered throughout the community or the world, they are still the church.

In the New Testament, the word translated *church* is used 115 times. Twenty-three times it refers to the church in general (all people who believe in Christ and follow Him). Ninety-two times *church* refers to a local body of baptized believers in a specific location. Members join together because of their common beliefs and mission.

The mission of every New Testament church should be threefold: 1) to share the gospel (good news) of Christ with every person; 2) to have fellowship and care for each member; and 3) to help each member become involved in the mission and work of the church. The primary reason to join a church is because you have accepted Christ as your Savior and want to be identified with Him. He died for the church and wants us to live for it.

You need to join a church because of the fellowship it provides. Through the support and encouragement received from church members, every Christian can be stronger in his or her faith. This fellowship includes worship, prayer, Bible study, training, and witnessing to others. Experiences in all of these will assure growth as a follower of Christ.

Many churches vary in the way they receive new members. The pastor of each church will be glad to answer questions and give counsel. New Christians become members by publicly stating their acceptance of Christ as Savior and formally applying for membership. This is usually followed by baptism. (And sometimes baptism serves as the entrance requirement.) Of course, baptism does not add to their salvation, but it is a visible symbol of their Christian experience. Others become members of local churches by "transfer of letter" from other churches of like faith. Sometimes when records are lost individuals are accepted on their statement of faith and previous church membership. However a person joins a church, it ought to be one of the most meaningful experiences of his or her life.

Prayer   *Father God, thank You for my church and the vital part it plays in my life and the life of my family. Church members have been my teachers, my exalters, and my support system. When I need to be encouraged, I know they'll be there. May You continue to strengthen the staff as they lead us. Amen.*

Action   Pray for your church leaders and members today. Write a letter to a member of the church staff to give him or her encouragement.

Reflections

Family life is full of major and minor crises—the ups and downs of health, success and failure in career, marriage, and divorce—and all kinds of characters. It is tied to places and events and histories. With all of these felt details, life etches itself into memory and personality. It's difficult to imagine anything more nourishing to the soul.

—THOMAS MOORE

□ □ □

Near to the Heart
of God

❧

When my anxious thoughts multiply within me,
Thy consolations delight my soul.

—PSALM 94:19

*L*ife is often filled with unexpected problems or crises. Unrest and despair will
darken the way of even the strongest
saint. Yet the Christian—because of the refuge he has in
God—should strive to maintain composure and stability
in spite of stress and difficulties. We cannot escape the
pressures and dark shadows in our lives, but they can be
faced with a spiritual strength that our Lord provides. As
we are held securely "near to the heart of God," we find
the rest, the comfort, the joy and peace that only Jesus our
Redeemer can give. Because of this, we can live every day
with an inner calm and courage.

This is the message that Cleland McAfee expressed
in this consoling hymn at a time when his own life was
filled with sadness. While he was serving as pastor of
the First Presbyterian Church in Chicago, Dr. McAfee was
stunned to hear the shocking news that his two beloved
nieces had just died from diphtheria. Turning to God and
the Scriptures, McAfee soon felt the lines and the tune of
this hymn flow from his grieving heart. On the day of the

double funeral, he stood outside the quarantined home of his brother Howard singing these words as he choked back the tears. The following Sunday the hymn was repeated by the choir of McAfee's church. It soon became widely known and has since ministered comfort and spiritual healing to many of God's people in times of need.

> There is a place of quiet rest, near to the heart of God, a place where sin cannot molest, near to the heart of God.
> There is a place of comfort sweet, near to the heart of God, a place where we our Savior meet, near to the heart of God.
> There is a place of full release, near to the heart of God, a place where all is joy and peace, near to the heart of God.
> *Chorus:* O Jesus, blest Redeemer, sent from the heart of God, hold us who wait before Thee near to the heart of God.[20]

Prayer

Father God, may I choose to live courageously, regardless of what may come my way. May I always be sensitive to Your nearness—a quiet rest, a place of comfort, and a place of full release.

Action

Write in your journal several episodes where God's nearness gave you comfort and strength.

Reflections

Enter as a Child

*Truly I say to you, unless you are converted
and become like children, you shall not enter
the kingdom of heaven.*

—MATTHEW 18:3

Our religion is one which challenges the ordinary human standards by holding that the ideal of life is the spirit of a little child. We tend to glorify adulthood and wisdom and worldly prudence, but the Gospel reverses all this. The Gospel says that the in-escapable condition of entrance into the divine fellowship is that we turn and become as a little child. As against our natural judgment we must become tender and full of wonder and unspoiled by the hard skepticism on which we so often pride ourselves. But when we really look into the heart of a child, willful as he may be, we are often ashamed. God has sent children into the world, not only to replenish it, but to serve as sacred reminders of something ineffably precious which we are always in danger of losing. The sacrament of childhood is thus a continuing education.[21]

—*Elton Trueblood*

One of the greatest gifts God has given me is to be able to spend quality time with my grandchildren. Not that those precious years with our children weren't stimulating—it's just that I wasn't wise enough to enjoy and appreciate my children as I do our grandchildren. Grandparenting is such a rewarding phase of life. We know more and are better able to understand and appreciate the wonderful gift of young children. They are so precious and innocent. I pray that they never leave the innocence of the Garden of Eden. Just by watching them, I learn so much about God. They reflect purity and guilelessness, trusting God with a faith so sincere.

Prayer   *Father God, may I appreciate You with the sincerity of a young child. May I appreciate the loveliest of your creation—a child. A baby is Your opinion that life should go on. May we not disappoint You as we raise them. Amen.*

Action   Try to pray to God in a childlike fashion— with utmost sincerity, trust, and faith.

Reflections

Friendship

*A friend loves at all times, and a brother
is born for adversity.*

—Proverbs 17:17

I have been so blessed with great friendships. I know not how I have accumulated
so many; at times they seem like puppies
hanging around a food bowl. They each have brought such
tenderness to my life and the joy of great anticipation when
we meet. Some friends just want to curl up around me and
cozy up to a warm blanket and enjoy the strokes I give them.
In return, they give me the nudge of their noses that tells me
they so enjoy our time together. On occasion, I have even given
my friends a time to doze on the couch and awaken again to
continue our time together. Friends are so warm and cuddly.

Henry Wadsworth Longfellow once wrote a poem that
expressed true love of friends and how they linger over a
period of years. It reads:

> I shot an arrow into the air,
> It fell to earth, I knew not where;
> For, so swiftly it flew, the sight
> Could not follow it in its flight.
>
> I breathed a song into the air,
> It fell to earth, I knew not where;

For who has sight so keen and strong,
That it can follow the flight of song?

Long, long afterward, in an oak
I found the arrow, still unbroke;
And the song, from beginning to end,
I found again in the heart of a friend.

—Henry Wadsworth Longfellow

Prayer   *Father God, what would I do without all my friends? They give me such support and strength. They are what gives my day purpose. May I, too, be a friend to my friends. Thank You for friendships. Amen.*

Action   Write a friend a thank-you note for welcoming you into her life.

Reflections

Worship

*Come let us worship and bow down; let us
kneel before the LORD our Maker.*

—PSALM 95:6

As people looked at the book of Psalms, they began to study the various forms of worship. As we look at the various denominations, we begin to see how the early founders of each established ways to worship by what they perceived after reading this great book. Over the centuries, Christian worship has taken many different forms, involving various expressions and postures on the part of the church goer. The beginning for many of these different expressions comes from the psalms, which portray worship as an act of the complete person, not just his mental sphere.

The Hebrew word for worship literally means "to kneel" or "to bow down." The act of worship is the gesture of humbling oneself before a higher authority.

The psalms also call upon us to "sing to the LORD, bless His name" (96:2). Music has always played a large part in this sacred facet of worship.

Physical gestures and movements are also mentioned. Lifting our hands before God signifies our loyalty to Him. Clapping our hands is representative of our celebrating before God. Some worshipers rejoice in His presence with tambourine and dancing (see Psalm 150:4).

To worship like the psalmists is to obey Jesus' command to "love the Lord your God with all your heart, and with all your soul, and with all your mind, and with all your strength" (Mark 12:30). There are several insights for worship in the book of Psalms:

- God's gifts of instruments and vocal music should be used to help us worship (Psalm 47:1; 81:1-4; 150)

- We can appeal to God for help and we can thank Him for His deliverance (4:3; 17:1-5)

- Difficult times should not prevent us from praising God (22:23,24; 102:1,2; 140:4-8)

- We are to celebrate what God has done for us (18; 106; 136)

- Confessing our sins relieves us of many burdens (32; 42:5-11; 116)

Prayer   *Father God, thank You for giving us the great book of Psalms, the great book of praise. There are so many ways to worship You. May I always stay open to these ways so I never think that my way alone is perfect. May all forms be acceptable to You. Amen.*

Action   Start your journey through the book of Psalms. Read chapters 1-3 today.

Reflections

Always Rejoice

Rejoice in the Lord always; again I will say, rejoice!

—PHILIPPIANS 4:4

In the Christian community we are often confused by this term *rejoice*. Often we equate it with our human idea of being happy. But happiness is something far less than the joy of rejoicing in the Lord. Martin Lloyd-Jones expresses this concept very well:

> We must recognize that there is all the difference in the world between rejoicing and feeling happy. The Scripture tells us that we should always rejoice. Take the lyrical Epistle of Paul to the Philippians where he says: "Rejoice in the Lord always and again I say rejoice." He goes on saying it. To rejoice is a command, yes, but there is all the difference in the world between rejoicing and being happy. You cannot make yourself happy, but you can make yourself rejoice, in the sense that you will always rejoice in the Lord. Happiness is something within ourselves, rejoicing is "in the Lord." How important it is then, to draw the distinction between rejoicing in the Lord and feeling happy. Take the fourth chapter of the Second Epistle to the Corinthians. There you will find that the great Apostle puts it all very plainly

and clearly in that series of extraordinary contrasts which he makes: "We are troubled on every side" (I don't think he felt very happy at the moment) "yet not distressed, we are perplexed" (he wasn't feeling happy at all at that point) "but not in despair," "persecuted but not forsaken," "cast down, but not destroyed"—and so on. In other words, the Apostle does not suggest a kind of happy person in a carnal sense, but he was still rejoicing. That is the difference between the two conditions.[22]

Prayer   *Father God, let me rejoice always, even in my lowest moments of life, for I know that these are rejoicings from You. Let me choose the higher road when difficult times come. Amen.*

Action   Write down several things you aren't happy about but in which you are also rejoicing. Why are you able to rejoice?

Reflections

Build Me a Son

Her children rise up and bless her.

—PROVERBS 31:28

There's something special about a son. A mother bonds so affectionately with her boys. God has given a tenderness there that lifts both a mother and her son, in many cases a stronger bond than with a daughter. Often a mother and daughter have to work out their competitive differences, but a godly mother seems to have that extra portion of love for her son.

General Douglas MacArthur once had a special prayer for his son. Even though it was written by a father to a son, it has also a particular meaning for a mother in raising a son. It reads:

> Build me a son, O Lord, who will be strong enough to know when he is weak, and brave enough to face himself when he is afraid; one who will be proud and unbending in honest defeat, and humble and gentle in victory.
>
> Build me a son whose wishbone will not be where his backbone should be; a son who will know thee and that to know himself is the foundation stone of knowledge.
>
> Lead him, I pray, not in the path of ease and comfort, but under the stress and spur of difficulties

217

and challenge. Here let him learn to stand up in the storm; here let him learn compassion for those who fail.

Build me a son whose heart will be clear, whose goal will be high; a son who will master himself before he seeks to master other men; one who will learn to laugh, yet never forget how to weep; one who will reach into the future, yet never forget the past.

And after all these things are his, add, I pray, enough of a sense of humor, so that he may always be serious, yet never take himself too seriously. Give him humility, so that he may always remember the simplicity of true greatness, the open mind of true wisdom, the meekness of true strength.

Then I, his father, will dare to whisper, "I have not lived in vain."[23]

Prayer   Father God, may You give me a special heart for raising a son. I sometimes feel so inadequate for this venture. Boys seem so rough and tough and here's little old me. I do want to be stretched in this assignment so that I can also say, "I have not lived in vain." Please give me added insight. Amen.

Action   Pray to God for a special blessing in trying to raise the future men in your family.

Reflection

Notes

1. Written by Paul Eaton, printed in the July 19, 1998 bulletin at Harvest Fellowship, Riverside, CA. Used by permission.

2. Taken from Fred Brock, *Hymns for the Family of God* (Nashville: Paragon Associates, 1976), p. 80.

3. Brian Culhane, comp., *The Treasure Chest* (New York: Harper Collins Publishers, 1995), p. 103.

4. Women's Devotional Bible (Grand Rapids, MI: Zondervan Corp., 1990), p. 321. Used by permission.

5. Ibid., p. 1260. Used by permission.

6. Culhane, *Treasure Chest*, p. 40.

7. Brock, *Hymns*, p. 615.

8. Women's Devotional Bible, p. 1048.

9. Kenneth W. Osbeck, comp., *Amazing Grace: 366 Hymn Stories for Personal Devotions,* (Grand Rapids, MI: Kregel Publications, 1990), p. 209. Used by permission.

10. This material is taken from *When Life Takes What Matters,* by Susan Lenzkes © 1993. Used by permission of Discovery House Publishers, Box 3566, Grand Rapids, MI 49501. All rights reserved.

11. Emilie Barnes, *Fill My Cup, Lord* (Eugene, OR: Harvest House, 1996, pp. 130-34.

12. Osbeck, *Amazing Grace*, p. 342.

13. Ibid., p. 221.

14. Source unknown.

15. Adapted from the Praise and Worship Study Bible (Wheaton, IL: Tyndale House Publishers, Inc., 1997).

16. Culhane, *Treasure Chest*. p. 92.

17. Ibid., p. 68.

18. Women's Devotional Bible, p. 1082.

19. Osbeck, *Amazing Grace*, p. 170.

20. Ibid., p. 281.

21. Culhane, *Treasure Chest*, p. 57.

22. Brock, *Hymns*, p. 47.

23. Culhane, *Treasure Chest*, p. 91.

For more information regarding speaking engagements and additional material, please send a self-addressed envelope to:

More Hours in My Day
2150 Whitestone Dr.
Riverside, CA 92506

Or you can visit us on the Internet at:
www.emiliebarnes.com
or
emilie@emiliebarnes.com

Harvest House Books by Bob & Emilie Barnes

Bob & Emilie Barnes

15-Minute Devotions
   for Couples
101 Ways to Love Your Grandkids
Be My Refuge, Lord
A Little Book of Manners
   for Boys
Minute Meditations
   for Couples

Bob Barnes

15 Minutes Alone
   with God for Men
500 Handy Hints for
   Every Husband
Men Under Construction
What Makes a Man
   Feel Loved

Emilie Barnes

The 15-Minute Organizer
15 Minutes Alone with God
15 Minutes of Peace
   with God
15 Minutes with God
   for Grandma
500 Time-Saving Hints
   for Women
Cleaning Up the Clutter
Designing Your Home on a Budget
Emilie's Creative
   Home Organizer
Everything I Know
   I Learned in My Garden
Everything I Know
   I Learned over Tea
Friendship Teas to Go

Garden Moment Getaways
A Grandma Is a Gift from God
Heal My Heart, Lord
Home Warming
If Teacups Could Talk
I Need Your Strength, Lord
An Invitation to Tea
Join Me for Tea
Journey Through Cancer
Keep It Simple
   for Busy Women
Let's Have a Tea Party!
A Little Book of Manners
A Little Hero in the Making
A Little Princess in the Making
The Little Teacup that Talked
Meet Me Where I Am, Lord
Minute Meditations
   for Busy Moms
Minute Meditations for Healing
   and Hope
More Faith in My Day
More Hours in My Day
One-Minute Home Organizer
Quiet Moments for
   a Busy Mom's Soul
A Quiet Refuge
Simple Secrets to
   a Beautiful Home
Survival for Busy Moms
A Tea to Comfort Your Soul
The Twelve Teas®
   of Celebration
The Twelve Teas®
   of Friendship
The Twelve Teas® of Inspiration
What Makes a Woman Feel Loved